MICROSOFT OFFICE
ACCESS 2003
QuickSteps

JOHN CRONAN

VIRGINIA ANDERSEN

BRENDA BRYANT ANDERSON

3/04

McGraw-Hill/Osborne

New York Chicago San Francisco
Lisbon London Madrid Mexico City
Milan New Delhi San Juan
Seoul Singapore Sydney Toronto

McGraw-Hill/Osborne

2100 Powell Street, 10th Floor
Emeryville, California 94608
U.S.A.

To arrange bulk purchase discounts for sales promotions, premiums, or fund-raisers, please contact **McGraw-Hill/ Osborne** at the above address. For information on translations or book distributors outside the U.S.A., please see the International Contact Information page immediately following the index of this book.

Microsoft®, PivotChart®, PivotTable®, SharePoint™, and Windows® are either registered trademarks or trademarks of Microsoft Corporation in the United States and/or other countries.

This book was composed with Adobe® InDesign®

Information has been obtained by **McGraw-Hill**/Osborne from sources believed to be reliable. However, because of the possibility of human or mechanical error by our sources, **McGraw-Hill**/Osborne, or others, **McGraw-Hill**/Osborne does not guarantee the accuracy, adequacy, or completeness of any information and is not responsible for any errors or omissions or the results obtained from use of such information.

MICROSOFT® OFFICE ACCESS 2003 QUICKSTEPS

1234567890 WCK WCK 01987654

ISBN 0-07-223229-3

PUBLISHER / Brandon A. Nordin

VICE PRESIDENT AND ASSOCIATE PUBLISHER / Scott Rogers

ACQUISITIONS EDITOR / Roger Stewart

ACQUISITIONS COORDINATOR / Jessica Wilson

TECHNICAL EDITORS / John Cronan, Brenda Bryant Anderson

COPY EDITOR / Chara Curtis

PROOFREADERS / Deborah Fisher, Kellen Diamanti

INDEXER / Deborah Fisher

LAYOUT ARTIST / Laura Canby

ILLUSTRATORS / Kathleen Edwards, Pattie Lee, Bruce Hopkins

SERIES DESIGN / Bailey Cunningham

COVER DESIGN / Pattie Lee

John Cronan:

To Faye Sturtevant, who in partnership with me disproved the popular notion that you can't go home again. Love ya, Baby.

Virginia Andersen:

To Grace Hopper, for introducing me to this wonderful world of computing back in 1948.

Brenda Bryant Anderson:

To Dana, love of my life, man of my dreams;

To Morgan and Chloe, the brightest stars and sweetest peas to ever exist; and

To Dad, for always doing whatever it took to help me succeed.

About the Authors

John Cronan:

John Cronan was introduced to computers when he was in college, over 25 years ago. John first became involved in writing and editing computer-related materials in the early 1990's. In the ensuing years, he has worked on dozens of books and software product manuals, additionally performing technical reviews of other authors' works in the course of operating his own technical writing and editing business. John recently wrote another book in this series, *Microsoft Office Excel 2003 QuickSteps*. Other recent books he has worked on and published by McGraw-Hill/Osborne include *Windows Server 2003: A Beginner's Guide*; *FrontPage 2003: The Complete Reference* (Matthews); and *Introduction to Windows 2003 Server* (Ecklund). John and his wife, Faye, (and cat, Little Buddy), live in historic Everett, WA.

Virginia Andersen:

Virginia Andersen became a writer and computer consultant after retiring from her defense contracting career. Since then, she has written or contributed to nearly 40 books about personal computer-based applications, including database management, word processing and spreadsheet analysis. Virginia spent nearly 15 years teaching computer science, mathematics, and systems analysis at the graduate and undergraduate levels at several Southern California universities. Recent books she has written and published by McGraw-Hill/Osborne include *Access 2003: The Complete Reference* and *How To Do Everything with Access 2003*.

Brenda Bryant Anderson:

Brenda Bryant Anderson has been involved in the computer industry for the past fourteen years. She spent most of this time with the Microsoft Corporation educating corporate customers and consultants on the uses of Microsoft software. For the last three years Brenda has taught a variety of college courses on software applications and their integration in the corporate arena. Brenda lives with her husband, Dana, and their two adorable daughters, Morgan and Chloe, in rural Washington State.

Contents at a Glance

Acknowledgments

Thanks so much to all…

Chara Curtis, copy editor, not only expertly combined the writing styles of three authors into one cohesive and consistent work but also provided a second set of eyes to the overall project management. Thanks, Chara, for keeping us in "step."

Laura Canby, layout artist, whose powers of alchemy blended black and white text with a plethora of varicolored art files to produce pure "gold." A great job, Laura, on a tight schedule and with nary a page out of "step."

John Cronan and **Brenda Bryant Anderson**, technical editors, who combined this role with their writing efforts, ensuring the technical accuracy of each chapter.

Deborah Fisher, indexer/proofreader, who found errors, large and small, and then "calmly" awaited our final writing so that she could produce the professional index we have.

Kellen Diamante, proofreader, for "stepping" to the plate and adding this responsibility to her own writing efforts. (Kellen is a co-author of *Microsoft Office Outlook 2003 QuickSteps*, published by McGraw-Hill/Osborne.)

Marty and **Carole Matthews**, series editors—whose vision, persistence, and just plain hard work provided all of us the opportunity to be members of this great QuickSteps team.

Contents

1

2

Conventions Used in this Book

Microsoft Office Access 2003 QuickSteps uses several conventions designed to make the book easier for you to follow. Among these are

- A 🔍 in the table of contents and in the How To list in each chapter references a QuickSteps sidebar in a chapter.

- **Bold type** is used for words or objects on the screen that you are to do something with—such as click **Save As**, open **File**, and click **Close**.

- *Italic type* is used for a word or phrase that is being defined or otherwise deserves special emphasis.

- Underlined type is used for text that you are to type on the keyboard.

- SMALL CAPITAL LETTERS are used for keys on the keyboard such as ENTER and SHIFT.

- When you are expected to enter a command, you are told to press the key(s). If you are to enter text or numbers, you are told to type them.

Introduction

QuickSteps books are recipe books for computer users. They answer the question "How do I…?" by providing quick sets of steps to accomplish the most common tasks with a particular program. The sets of steps are the central focus of the book. QuickSteps sidebars show you how to quickly do many small functions or tasks that support primary functions. Notes, Tips, and Cautions augment the steps, yet they are presented in such a manner so as to not interrupt the flow of the steps. The brief introductions are minimal rather than narrative, and numerous illustrations and figures, many with callouts, support the steps.

QuickSteps books are organized by function and the tasks needed to perform that function. Each function is a chapter. Each task, or "How To," contains the steps needed for accomplishing the function along with the relevant Notes, Tips, Cautions, and screenshots. Tasks will be easy to find through:

- The table of contents, which lists the functional areas (chapters) and tasks in the order they are presented

- A How To list of tasks on the opening page of each chapter

- The index, which provides an alphabetical list of the terms that are used to describe the functions and tasks

- Color-coded tabs for each chapter or functional area with an index to the tabs in the Contents at a Glance

Chapter 1
Stepping into Access

This chapter explains how to load Access, open a database file, interpret its window, and then personalize settings to meet your own needs. You will learn how to get help, online and offline, and to use the Office Assistant. This chapter will also show you how to end an Access session.

Start Access

I assume that you already know how to turn on the computer and load Windows and that Access has been installed on your computer. Once Access is installed, you may start it as you would any other program—using the Start menu, using the keyboard, and using shortcuts you have created. Existing Access databases can be opened in similar ways, and recently used databases can be quickly opened from within Access.

Many programs, such as Microsoft Office Excel and Word, open with a new, blank file ready for you to start entering text or data. Access does not do this, as you are more likely to use a wizard to assist you in setting up a new database. You will see how to open existing databases later in this chapter and how to create new databases in Chapter 2.

QUICKSTEPS

Use the Start Menu to Start Access

Normally, the surest way to start Access is to use the Start menu.

1. Start your computer if it is not running, and log on to Windows if necessary.

2. Click **Start**. The Start menu opens.

3. Either:

   - Click **Microsoft Office Access 2003** in the lower half of the Start menu. Programs you've opened recently will be listed here.

   –Or–

   - Select **All Programs**, choose **Microsoft Office**, and click **Microsoft Office Access 2003**.

In either case, the Access window opens with the Getting Started task pane displayed, as shown in Figure 1-1.

Figure 1-1: The Access window doesn't really come to life until you open a database.

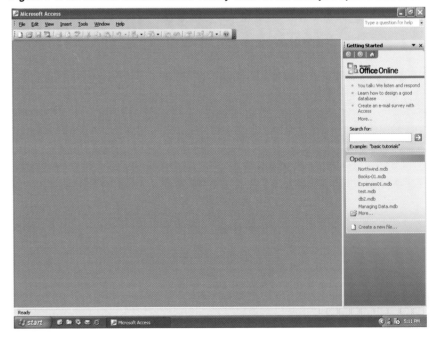

Tour the Database Window

The container for data and the Access objects that manage the data is a file called a Microsoft Office Access Database that includes an .mdb file extension, for example, MyDatabase.mdb. A *database* in its simplest form is just a collection, or list, of data on a related subject—for example, the pertinent information on a publisher's books, such as the title, author, ISBN number, selling price, and the number of books sold and on order.

A database can contain a single collection of data, or it can be divided among sub-collections that are related by common categories. A database can also be utilized at different roles. You can be a database *user*, who adds and/or retrieves data, such as account information in a large corporate system. Or you can be a database *designer*, who creates the structure of the database for others to use. In most cases you're a bit of both: for example, you might create your own design for keeping track of your music collection and enter the information yourself.

When a database is first opened you see the "Grand Central Station" of Access—the Database window displayed within the Access window, as shown in Figure 1-2. From within this framework you can open, create, design, and remove the components, or *objects*, that comprise a database. These seven objects let you store, find, enter, present, and manipulate your data:

- **Tables** contain data, organized by categories called *field*s, into unique sets of data called *records*.

- **Queries** are requests you make of your data to extract just the information you want or to perform maintenance actions, such as inserting or deleting records.

- **Forms** provide a user-friendly interface for entering or displaying data.

- **Reports** allow you to take mundane collections of data, organize them in a creative package, and print the result.

- **Pages** extend the reach of Access data entering and display facilities for use on the Internet and internal intranets.

- **Macros** provide a means to automate actions in Access without in-depth programming skills.

NOTE

Another Access database file, a *project* or .adp file, does not contain data but is used to connect to the data in a Microsoft SQL (structured query language) Server database. Using projects and connecting to SQL Server databases are advanced topics outside the scope of this book.

Figure 1-2: The Access window provides a framework to support the objects that are opened or created from the Database window.

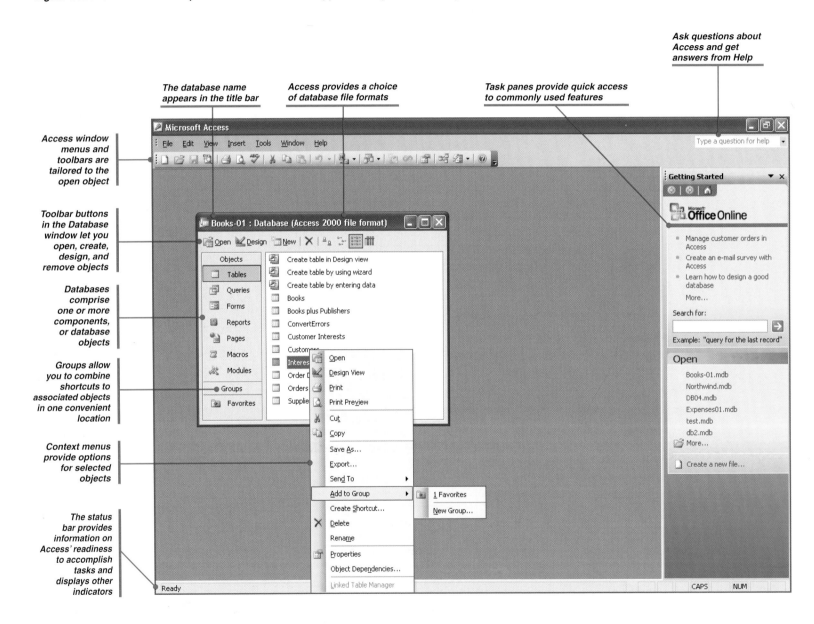

Ask questions about Access and get answers from Help

The database name appears in the title bar

Access provides a choice of database file formats

Task panes provide quick access to commonly used features

Access window menus and toolbars are tailored to the open object

Toolbar buttons in the Database window let you open, create, design, and remove objects

Databases comprise one or more components, or database objects

Groups allow you to combine shortcuts to associated objects in one convenient location

Context menus provide options for selected objects

The status bar provides information on Access' readiness to accomplish tasks and displays other indicators

- **Modules** package Visual Basic code into a single container, providing a convenient interface for coupling Access to the possibilities offered by a programming language.

The remaining chapters in this book describe these objects in more detail.

Open a Database

You open an Access database by locating the database .mdb file. You can manually find the database file using a dialog box, task pane, shortcut, or Windows Explorer. (If you do not know the location of the file, you can do a search on your drives, as described in "Find a Database.") For files you have previously opened, Windows and Access provide a number of aids you can use to reopen them quickly.

Figure 1-3: To stay one step ahead of potential problems from malicious code, you should install the latest security updates to Access and your operating system.

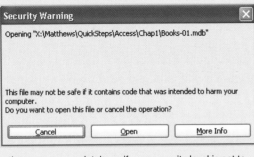

NOTE

Databases can contain code that could cause serious harm to your computer. To alert you to this potential problem, a Security Warning dialog box will open every

Security Warning

Opening "X:\Matthews\QuickSteps\Access\Chap1\Books-01.mdb"

This file may not be safe if it contains code that was intended to harm your computer.
Do you want to open this file or cancel the operation?

| Cancel | Open | More Info |

time you open a database if your security level is set to High or Medium. Though I don't recommend it, if you trust the sources of your data and don't want or need the security reminder, you can eliminate the security warning by lowering your security level. Click the **Tools** menu, point at **Macro**, and select **Security**. In the Security dialog box, select **Low**. Click **OK** to close the dialog box. See Chapter 9 for more information on database security.

Low (not recommended). You are not protected from potentially unsafe macros. Use this setting only if you have virus scanning software installed, or you have checked the safety of all documents you open.

USE A DIALOG BOX TO OPEN A DATABASE

To open a database with the Open dialog box:

1. Start Access.

2. Click the **File** menu and select **Open**, or click **Open** on the Database toolbar.

3. In the Open dialog box, shown in Figure 1-4, you can open the **Look In** drop-down list to begin your search; or you can click **My Recent Documents**, **Desktop**, **My Documents**, **My Computer**, or **My Network Places**, and then browse until you find the database you want.

4. When you have located it, double-click the database file to open it, or select it and click **Open**.

Figure 1-4: The Open dialog box allows you to browse to find a database file.

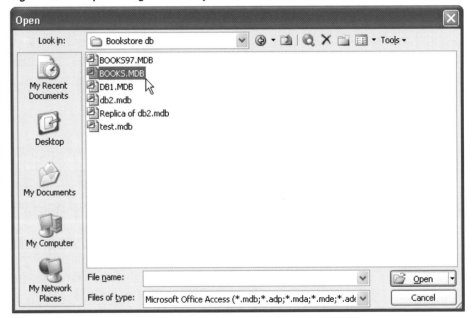

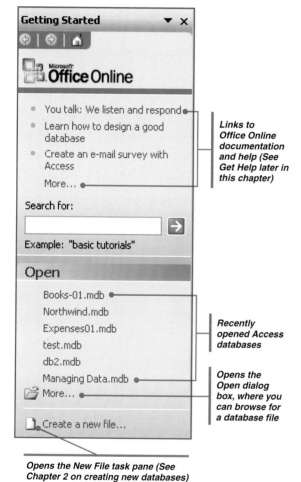

Figure 1-5: The Getting Started task pane lists links to recently opened databases and to other useful locations.

Links to Office Online documentation and help (See Get Help later in this chapter)

Recently opened Access databases

Opens the Open dialog box, where you can browse for a database file

Opens the New File task pane (See Chapter 2 on creating new databases)

OPEN RECENTLY USED DATABASES

Start Access and choose from three methods:

- Click the **File** menu and select a database from the bottom of the menu.

  1 Books-01.mdb

  2 C:\Program Files\...\Northwind.mdb

  3 C:\...\Expenses01.mdb

  4 \Matthews\QuickSteps\Access\...\test.mdb

  5 \Matthews\QuickSteps\Access\...\db2.mdb

  6 \Matthews\...\Managing Data.mdb

  Exit

- Press **CTRL+O** to open the Open dialog box (see "Use a Dialog Box to Open a Database" earlier in this chapter), and click **My Recent Documents** in the sidebar on the left of the dialog box.

- Display the Getting Started task pane (see the "Using Task Panes" QuickSteps for more information on working with task panes), and in the Open area, click one of the recently used databases, as shown in Figure 1-5.

USE WINDOWS EXPLORER TO OPEN A DATABASE

1. Open **Start** and click **My Computer**. Depending on your settings, you may see a tasks pane or a folders pane on the left of the My Computer window. If necessary, click **Folders** on the toolbar to display a folders list in the left pane.

2. Open one of the default folders, such as My Documents or Shared Documents; or under My Computer, open the drive and folder(s) that contain the database you want to open. When you open the folder that contains the database in the left pane, the database file will be displayed in the right pane.

3. Double-click the file name, as shown in Figure 1-6, to open the database in Access.

TIP

You can change how many recently used database files appear at the bottom of the File menu and in the Open area of the Getting Started task pane. Open a database, click the **Tools** menu, select **Options**, and click the **General** tab. Ensure the **Recently Used File List** check box is selected, and then click the **down arrow** next to it to select how many files you want to list. Click **OK** when finished.

☑ Recently used file list: 6 ▾

TIP

Windows keeps track of your most recently used documents, including Access database files. Click **Start**, point at **My Recent Documents**, and click the database file you want to open. If you do not have a My Recent Documents menu, right-click **Start**, and select **Properties**. In the Taskbar And Start Menu Properties dialog box, select **Customize**, click the **Advanced** tab, and select the **List My Most Recently Opened Documents** check box. Click **OK** twice to close all open dialog boxes.

☑ List my most recently opened documents

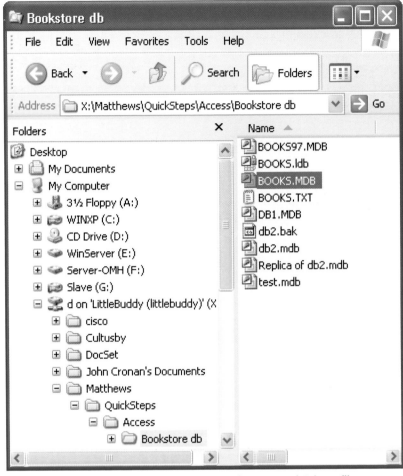

Figure 1-6: Use Windows Explorer to locate and open any database file on your computer or network.

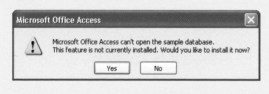

TIP

To open the sample database that's included with your installation of Access, click the **Help** menu, point at **Sample Databases**, and select **Northwind Sample Database**. Depending on how Access was set up, you might need to install the database. Click **Yes** in the dialog box to install the database, and then click **Open** in the Security Warning dialog box.

CAUTION

Back up any Access database file before you try to convert it! See Chapter 9 to learn how to administer databases.

CREATE SHORTCUTS TO OPEN A DATABASE

Just as you can create a shortcut to start Access, you can create a shortcut to a database file. Opening the file will open the database in Access, starting Access if it isn't already open.

1. Locate the database file as described in the previous section, "Use Windows Explorer to Open a Database."

2. Click the file using the right mouse button, and drag it to:

   - The upper-left corner of the Start menu

   - The desktop

   - The Quick Launch toolbar

   - Another folder

3. Release the mouse button, and click **Create Shortcuts Here** from the context menu if it is displayed.

Open Older Databases

If you try to open an Access database created in versions prior to Access 2000, you will be presented with the option of *converting* (updating) the database to the default file format you currently have chosen or opening it using its native format.

1. Open the database using the techniques described in "Open a Database." The Convert/Open Database dialog box, shown in Figure 1-7, opens.

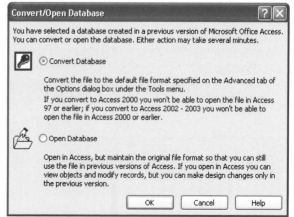

Figure 1-7: When opening Access databases created prior to Access 2000, you can choose to convert them to a newer file format or to keep them in their original format.

NOTE

Access 2003 might not have converters for very early Access versions. If you are informed you need to install a converter and cannot find one on the Microsoft Office web site, you might have to request one from Microsoft. Go to http://support.microsoft.com, click the **Contact Microsoft** link, and submit a request.

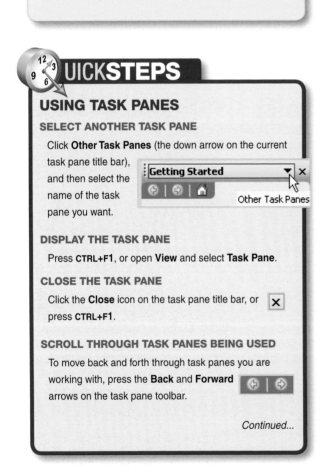

QUICKSTEPS

USING TASK PANES

SELECT ANOTHER TASK PANE

Click **Other Task Panes** (the down arrow on the current task pane title bar), and then select the name of the task pane you want.

DISPLAY THE TASK PANE

Press **CTRL+F1**, or open **View** and select **Task Pane**.

CLOSE THE TASK PANE

Click the **Close** icon on the task pane title bar, or press **CTRL+F1**.

SCROLL THROUGH TASK PANES BEING USED

To move back and forth through task panes you are working with, press the **Back** and **Forward** arrows on the task pane toolbar.

Continued...

2. Select:

- **Convert Database** if you want to permanently change the file to your default Access file format. Doing so will prevent the database from being opened by earlier Access versions. (See the next section, "Change the Default Access File Format.")

- **Open Database** if you want to open the database in its original file format. Doing so limits your ability to use many newer Access features. Most notably, you won't be able to change the structure (design) of the database.

3. Click **OK**.

Change the Default Access File Format

The Access database file format changes somewhat in each newly released version to accommodate new features and provide better security. However, Access is not generally *forward compatible*, meaning that older versions of Access cannot recognize newer file formats without converting them to the older file format (if that's even possible). By default, Access 2003 uses the Access 2000 file format, ensuring that your database files can be opened by users who have Access 2000 and later. You can change the default file format to Access 2002-2003. The advantages to using the new file format (improved storage, allowances for possible future changes, and the ability to save compiled modules) generally don't outweigh the flexibility offered by using the Access 2000 file format.

1. Open an Access database.

2. Click the **Tools** menu, select **Options**, and click the **Advanced** tab.

3. Under Default File Format, click the **down arrow** and select **Access 2002-2003**.

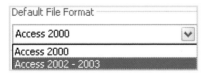

4. Click **OK** when finished.

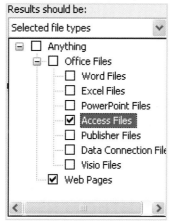
TIP

All forms of a word typed into Search Text are searched for. For example, searching a database that has the word "account" will find files containing "account," "accounting," and "accounted." If you cannot find your database using the basic search techniques, click **Advanced File Search** on the Basic File Search task pane for more options.

Find a Database

To find a database whose name and location you have forgotten, although you remember other information about it:

1. Click the **File** menu and select **File Search**. The Basic File Search task pane opens, as shown in Figure 1-8.

2. In **Search Text**, type words you know are contained in the database or keywords (words or phrases associated with the database). See Chapter 2 for ways to add identifying information to a database file.

3. Open **Search In**, and select a location to narrow the scope of your search.

4. Open **Results Should Be**, and *deselect* all check boxes except Access Files.

5. Click **Go**.

Figure 1-8: The Basic File Search task pane provides options for common search techniques and a link to more advanced features.

NOTE

Searching by Access takes advantage of the Indexing Service provided by Windows XP and other Windows operating systems, resulting in much faster searches of disks and drives. The Indexing Service is not started by default, so you need to manually start it, and it is recommended you do so. To start the Indexing Service, open **Start**, right-click **My Computer**, and click **Manage**. Open **Service And Applications**, and select **Indexing Service**. Open **Action** and select **Start**.

Personalize Access

You can personalize how you work with Access by choosing to display task panes, customizing toolbars and menus, and rearranging windows.

Remove the Getting Started Task Pane

When you start Access, the Getting Started task pane automatically appears. To hide it:

1. Open a database.
2. Click the **Tools** menu, select **Options**, and click the **View** tab to open it.
3. Under Show, click **Startup Task Pane** to remove the check mark ☐ Startup Task Pane in its check box.
4. Click **OK** when finished.

Select a Toolbar to Display

At first glance in the Database window, you appear to have a very limited inventory of toolbars at your disposal. However, as you work with tables, forms, and reports, you will find there are several more toolbars in Access that become available only when you have the pertinent object opened.

To display a toolbar:

1. Open **View** and select **Toolbars**. The Toolbars menu will be displayed with a tailored list of toolbars that pertain to the opened object or current task.
2. Click the toolbar you want to display. A check mark is placed next to it, and the toolbar displays on the screen.

NOTE

As you drag the command from the dialog box to the toolbar, it will initially drag a small rectangle containing an "X," signifying a placement cannot be made where it is. The rectangle will change into a plus sign, signifying a copy, when the pointer is over the toolbars, and then into an I-beam icon over the individual icons. This I-beam icon marks the insertion point where the command icon will be inserted between the adjoining icons on the toolbar.

TIP

The steps in "Add Commands to the Toolbar" and the Note above can be used for adding commands to a menu. Don't worry about messing things up. You can always click **Reset Menu And Toolbar Usage Data** on the Options tab of the Customize menu to restore the menus and toolbars to default settings.

Customize a Toolbar

You can customize a toolbar or menu by adding commands or menus to it or by creating a new toolbar and adding commands to that.

ADD COMMANDS TO THE TOOLBAR

If you find the buttons on the toolbars are not as convenient as you would like, or if you frequently use a feature that is not on one of the toolbars, you can rearrange the buttons or add commands to a toolbar.

1. Click the **Tools** menu, choose **Customize**, and select the **Commands** tab.
2. Under Categories, select the category where the command will be found.
3. Under Commands, find the command, and drag it from the dialog box to the location on the toolbar where you want it.
4. Click **Close** when you are finished.

CREATE A CUSTOM TOOLBAR

You can create a custom toolbar with the commands on it that you most frequently use, avoid displaying several toolbars, and make more open space for the object window.

1. Click the **Tools** menu, choose **Customize**, and select the **Toolbars** tab.
2. Click **New**. The New Toolbar dialog box will be displayed:

3. Type the name of the new toolbar, and click **OK**. A small toolbar will appear on the screen with the first few letters of its name in the title bar.
4. Use the steps in "Add Commands to the Toolbar" to build the toolbar with the commands you want.

UICKSTEPS

USING TOOLBARS

DISPLAY A TOOLBAR

Right-click a toolbar or the menu bar, and click the toolbar you want to be displayed.

MOVE A TOOLBAR

- When the toolbar is docked (attached to the edge of a window), place your pointer on the handle on the left of the toolbar, and drag it to the new location.
- When the toolbar is floating, place your pointer on the title bar of the toolbar, and drag it to the new location.

HIDE A TOOLBAR

1. Right-click the toolbar.
2. Click the toolbar to remove the check mark.

DELETE A TOOLBAR

You can delete only custom toolbars that you have created.

1. Open **Tools**, select **Customize**, and click the **Toolbars** tab.
2. Click the check box next to the toolbar you want to delete.
3. Click **Delete**. You will be asked if you really want to delete the toolbar.
4. Click **OK** and click **Close**.

DRAG A MENU TO A TOOLBAR

Access provides several menus you can add to a custom or existing toolbar.

1. Click the **Tools** menu and select **Customize**.
2. Click the **Commands** tab, and select **Built-in Menus** from the Categories list.
3. Drag the menu you want to the destination toolbar. See "Add Commands to the Toolbar," earlier in this chapter, for steps on how to move commands.

Show Full Menus

Microsoft Office products are installed by default with short menus that show the most commonly used commands and then require you to click double-chevrons or linger your pointer on the menu to expand it. You can choose to have the full list of commands displayed when you open an Access menu.

1. Open a database.
2. Click the **Tools** menu, select **Customize**, and click the **Options** tab.
3. In the Personalized Menus And Toolbars area, select the **Always Show Full Menus** check box.

   ☑ Always show full menus

4. Click **Close** when finished.

TIP

When you drag a toolbar next to the edge of the window, it will automatically attach itself to the window and become docked.

QUICKSTEPS

USING THE KEYBOARD IN ACCESS

Though most of us live and die by our mouse while using our computers, there isn't much in Access that can't also be done from the keyboard. Here's a summary of the actions described in this chapter.

USE THE START MENU

1. Press the **Windows flag key** on the bottom row of your keyboard, or press **CTRL+ESC**.

2. Use the arrow keys to move to the item you want.

3. Press **ENTER**.

OPEN A DATABASE

1. Press **CTRL+O**.

2. Press **TAB** to move between the various controls in the window and the arrow keys to select drives and folders.

3. Press **ENTER** to open folders and the arrows key to select the database file.

4. Press **ENTER** to open the database in Access.

OPEN A MENU AND SELECT A COMMAND

1. Press **ALT+** the underlined letter in the menu name you want.

2. Press **DOWN ARROW** until the command you want is selected.

3. Press **ENTER**.

OPEN THE GETTING STARTED TASK PANE

Press **CTRL+F1**.

CLOSE A DATABASE

Select the Database window and press **CTRL+F4**.

CLOSE ACCESS

Press **ALT+F4**.

View Shortcut Keys

You can display the shortcut keys for toolbar buttons that have them (for example, CTRL+O for the Open button).

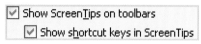

1. Open a database.

2. Open **Tools**, select **Customize**, and click the **Options** tab.

3. In the Other area, select the **Show ScreenTips On Toolbars** and **Show Shortcut Keys In ScreenTips** check boxes.

> ☑ Show ScreenTips on toolbars
> ☑ Show shortcut keys in ScreenTips

4. Click **Close** when finished.

Rearrange Object Windows

Although you can only have one database open at a time, you can have several Access objects opened in their own windows.

RESIZE OBJECT WINDOWS

1. Click the title bar of the window you want to resize to make it the active window.

2. Place your mouse pointer on top of the window border until it changes to a double-headed arrow.

   - To change the window size in one dimension, drag the window border toward or away from the center of the window.

   - To change the window size in two dimensions, drag a window corner toward or away from the center of the window.

USING THE KEYBOARD IN WINDOWS

Some keyboard commands are applicable to Windows programs in general.

USE THE START MENU

1. Press the **Windows flag key** on the bottom row of your keyboard, or press **CTRL+ESC**.
2. Use the arrow keys to move to the item you want.
3. Press **ENTER**.

MOVE A WINDOW

1. Press **ALT+SPACEBAR** to open the Control Box menu in the upper left of the window.
2. Press **DOWN ARROW** to select **Move**, and press **ENTER**.
3. Press one of the four arrow keys to move the window in the direction of the arrow.
4. Press **ESC** when finished.

RESIZE A WINDOW

1. Press **ALT+SPACEBAR** to open the Control menu in the upper left of the window.

2. Press **DOWN ARROW** to select **Size**, and press **ENTER**.
3. Press the arrow key that corresponds to the border you want to size from. A double-headed sizing arrow will be placed on that border.

4. Press the arrow key that corresponds to the direction you want to size the window.
5. Press **ESC** when finished.

MOVE OBJECT WINDOWS

Drag the title bar of the window you want to move.

SHRINK/EXPAND OBJECT WINDOWS

Click the **Minimize** button in the title bar.

The object window will shrink down so just a portion of the title bar appears at the bottom of the Access window and also as a task on the Windows taskbar.

To unhide the window, click the **Restore Up** button on the title bar or click the task on the taskbar.

DISPLAY AN OBJECT WINDOW AT ITS MAXIMUM SIZE

Click the **Maximize** button in the window title bar. To minimize the window or restore it to its previous size, use the set of buttons below those for the Access window itself in the upper-right corner of the Access window.

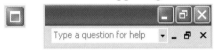

HIDE/UNHIDE OBJECT WINDOWS

1. Select the window you want to hide.
2. Click the **Window** menu and select **Hide**. The window "disappears." Repeat for any other windows you want to hide.
3. To unhide a window, click the **Window** menu and select **Unhide**. Select the window to be unhidden in the **Unhide Window** dialog box, and click **OK**.

ARRANGE MULTIPLE OBJECT WINDOWS

With two or more object windows open in Access, click the Window menu and select:

- **Tile Horizontally** to fill the database window with horizontal panes comprised of however many open windows you have

- **Tile Vertically** to fill the database window with vertical panes comprised of however many open windows you have

- **Cascade** to align the open windows in an overlapping stack (as shown in Figure 1-9)

Figure 1-9: You can arrange open object windows horizontally, vertically, or in an overlapping stack.

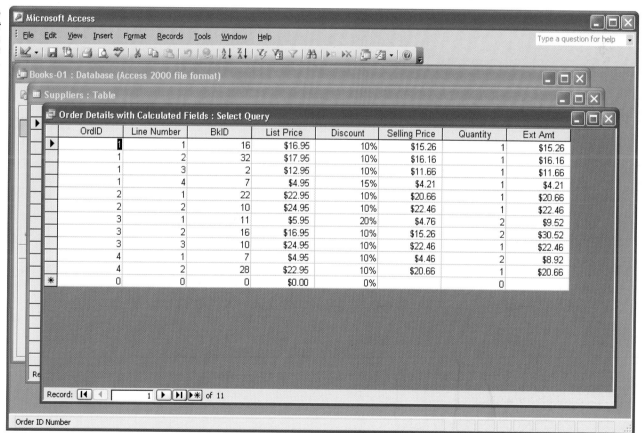

QUICKSTEPS

USING HELP

PRINT A HELP TOPIC

Click the **Print** icon in the Help topic dialog box toolbar.

HIDE/SHOW THE OFFICE ASSISTANT

The Office Assistant (named Clippit) provides hints and other assistance as you work in Access.

Open **Help** and select either **Hide The Office Assistant** or **Show The Office Assistant,** depending on whether you want to hide or show it.

CHANGE OFFICE ASSISTANTS

1. Right-click the current **Office Assistant**, and click **Choose Assistant** on the context menu.

2. In the Gallery tab of the Office Assistant dialog box, click the **Next** button several times to cycle through the available assistants and read their descriptions, as shown in Figure 1-11.

   Hide

   Options...

   Choose Assistant...

   Animate!

3. Click **OK** when you have the "new hire" you want displayed.

CHOOSE WHAT TIPS OFFICE ASSISTANT OFFERS

1. Right-click the **Office Assistant**, and click **Options** on the context menu.

2. Select the options you want by clicking them and placing a check mark in their respective check boxes.

3. Click **OK** when finished.

LIVEN UP YOUR OFFICE ASSISTANT

By default your Office Assistant is a bit of a couch potato—sort of just hangs out. To get him/her moving, right-click the static **Office Assistant**, and click **Animate!** on the context menu.

Get Help

Microsoft provides a vast amount of assistance to Access users. Automatically sensing whether there is an Internet connection, Access tailors much of the assistance offered to whether you are working online or offline.

Open Help

You are never far from help on Access.

DISPLAY THE ACCESS HELP TASK PANE

The Access Help task pane, shown in Figure 1-10, provides links to several assistance tools and forums, including a table of contents, access to downloads, contact information, and late-breaking news on Access.

- Click the **Help** menu, and select **Microsoft Office Access Help**.

  –Or–

- Click the **Microsoft Office Access Help** icon on the Database toolbar.

  –Or–

- Press **F1**.

Figure 1-10: The Access Help task pane provides links to several avenues of online and offline assistance.

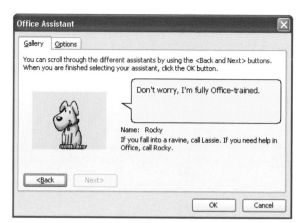

Figure 1-11: You can choose an Office Assistant more to your liking than the default Clippit.

ASK A QUESTION

You can quickly ask questions about Access directly from the menu bar without use of the Access Help task pane.

1. Type the question you want answered in the **Type A Question For Help** text box.

2. Press **ENTER**.

HIDE THE TYPE A QUESTION FOR HELP BOX

To remove the display of the Type A Question For Help box:

1. Click the **Tools** menu and select **Customize**.

2. With the Customize dialog box open, right-click the **Type A Question For Help** box on the menu bar.

3. Click the check mark beside the **Show Ask A Question** box, removing the check mark.

4. Click **Close** on the dialog box. When the dialog box is closed, the text box will be removed from the menu bar.

End Your Access Session

Changes that require saving are made as you work in the database object level, such as when you change the design of a table. Therefore, you don't need to "save" a database when you exit, as you would a typical file, such as a Word document.

Close a Database

If you want to close a database and keep Access open for work with other databases, use this procedure. Otherwise, to close the database and close Access in one step, do the procedure in "Close Access."

Click **Close** in the Database window (see Figure 1-12), or press **CTRL+F4**.

Close Access

Click **Close** in the Access window (see Figure 1-12), or press **ALT+F4**.

Figure 1-12: Changes to the database are saved as you work in the database object you have open. You close a database or Access by simply clicking their respective Close buttons.

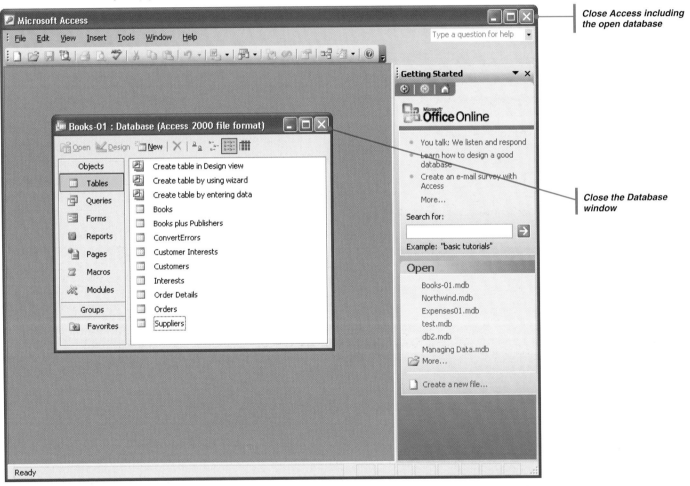

Close Access including the open database

Close the Database window

Chapter 2
Creating a Database

Access provides some great tools to assist in the creation of a turnkey database solution.

These tools expedite the building process but might rob you of the experience to better understand database structure. If speed is what you want, this chapter will show you how to use Access' Database Wizard or the samples from Office Online to quickly create an Access database. If, however, you choose to obtain a more thorough understanding of databases, you will learn how to step through the building process. That process includes basic database design, table creation, and table connections through relationships.

Create the Database Framework

Databases are created to provide quick, easy access to information. The data, or information, is stored in tables that resemble spreadsheets, as shown in Figure 2-1. They have columns, or *fields*, which span the vertical space of the window; and rows, or *records*, which cover the horizontal area of the window.

After creating the tables, forms can be made to ease the task of data entry. You can ask questions, or create *queries*, about the data stored in the database and generate reports to attractively display the information from your tables or queries.

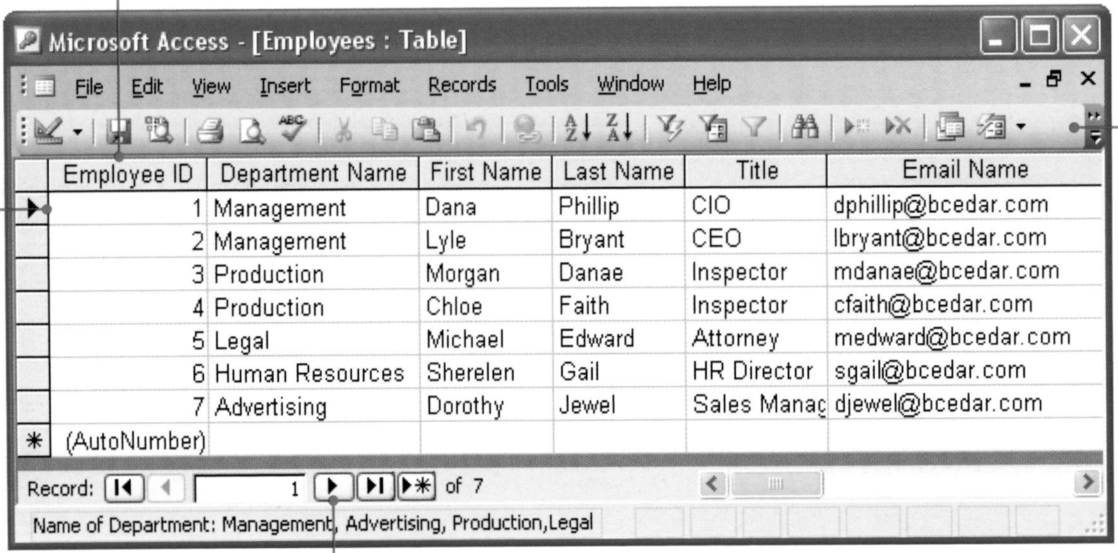

Columns, or fields, contain different kinds of information about the subject.

Rows, or records, contain all the information about one person, thing, or place.

Access toolbars change depending on the object selected.

Microsoft Access - [Employees : Table]

File   Edit   View   Insert   Format   Records   Tools   Window   Help

Employee ID	Department Name	First Name	Last Name	Title	Email Name
▶ 1	Management	Dana	Phillip	CIO	dphillip@bcedar.com
2	Management	Lyle	Bryant	CEO	lbryant@bcedar.com
3	Production	Morgan	Danae	Inspector	mdanae@bcedar.com
4	Production	Chloe	Faith	Inspector	cfaith@bcedar.com
5	Legal	Michael	Edward	Attorney	medward@bcedar.com
6	Human Resources	Sherelen	Gail	HR Director	sgail@bcedar.com
7	Advertising	Dorothy	Jewel	Sales Manag	djewel@bcedar.com
* (AutoNumber)					

Record: ◄ ◄ 1 ► ►I ►* of 7

Name of Department: Management, Advertising, Production, Legal

Figure 2-1: Access tables resemble spreadsheets and are the core containers of information.

Easy navigation buttons help you reach specific records quickly.

Figure 2-2: The New File task pane
provides shortcuts to templates.

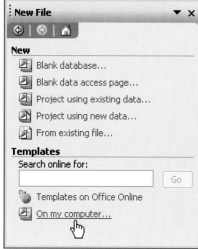

Figure 2-2: The New File task pane
provides shortcuts to templates.

Use a Database Template

There are many ways to create an Access database. The first and easiest way is to use one of the ten templates included in Access. The templates launch a database wizard that walks you through the creation of fairly complex databases. Once created, you can edit the database to customize its structure.

1. Open Access using one of the procedures described in Chapter 1.

2. If the New File task pane isn't visible, click the **File** menu and select **New**. The New File task pane opens to the right of the Access window. In the New File task pane (shown in Figure 2-2), under Templates, click **On My Computer**.

3. Click the **Databases** tab. You will see ten commonly created databases. As you select the different templates, a graphic representation of each is displayed on the right side of the dialog box, as shown in Figure 2-3.

Figure 2-3: Quickstart your database creation using pre-existing templates.

Select the General tab to create blank databases.

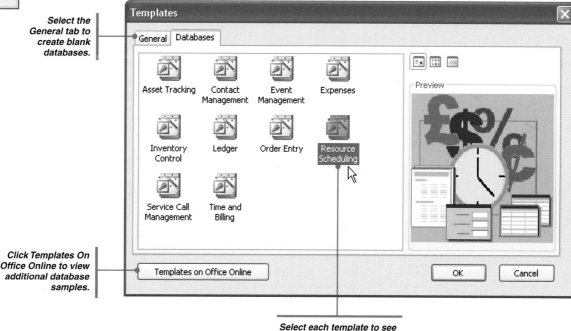

Click Templates On Office Online to view additional database samples.

Select each template to see a graphic representation.

4. Select a template and click **OK**. The File New Database dialog box will be displayed.

5. Type a file name for your database, or use the default name already in the File Name text box. Browse to the folder in which you want your new database located. Click the **Create** button to launch the Database Wizard.

SELECT TABLES AND FIELDS

The Database Wizard takes you through six basic steps. The first provides a description of the template, allowing you to cancel the wizard if it's not what you want. The second lets you add optional fields.

1. In the first Database Wizard dialog box, click **Next** to continue with the database template as described.

2. In the second screen, select each table to view the corresponding fields. Some tables have optional italicized fields, as shown in Figure 2-4. Click the check box next to the italicized field name to include it in the table. Click **Next**.

TIP

If the Back button at the bottom of the Database Wizard's window is not grayed, you can go back through previous steps in the wizard and change your selections.

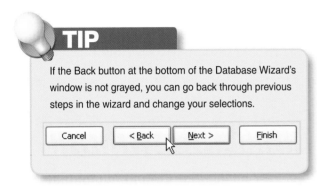

Select each table to view the corresponding fields.

Scroll to the bottom of the lists to see optional fields.

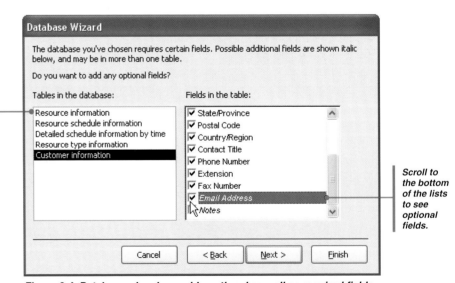

Figure 2-4: Database wizards provide optional as well as required fields.

CUSTOMIZE THE LOOK OF YOUR FORMS AND REPORTS

In steps 3 and 4 of the Database Wizard, you choose the graphic styles for your forms and printed reports. Select the descriptions to view the examples, as shown in Figure 2-5. Choose the style that fits your design needs, and click **Next** after each selection.

Select graphic descriptions to see samples to the left.

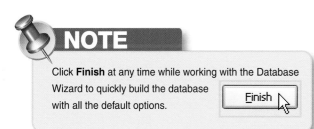

NOTE

Click **Finish** at any time while working with the Database Wizard to quickly build the database with all the default options.

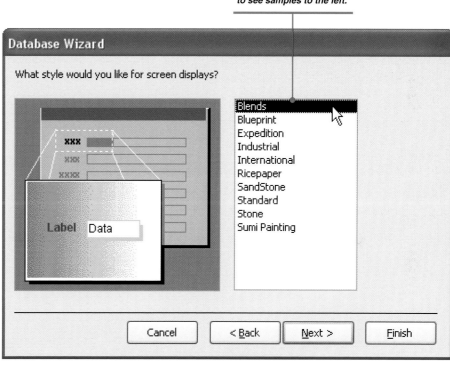

Figure 2-5: Graphics for forms can enhance database appearance.

CREATE DATABASE TITLE

The Database Wizard's fifth step lets you specify the title that will appear on the Access title bar. You can also choose if you want to include a picture in your reports.

1. Accept the default title or type a new one in the screen's text box.

2. To include a picture on your reports, select the **check box**.

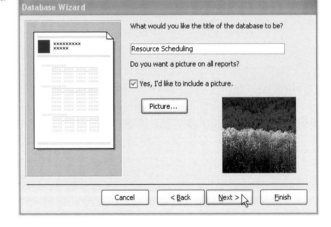

3. Click **Picture** to insert a picture from your computer. In the picture dialog box, browse your computer for the picture you wish to insert. The picture file format allows most commonly used graphic types. For more information on working with pictures, see Chapter 8.

4. Select your picture and click **OK**. Your picture will be displayed in the Database Wizard dialog box. Click **Next**.

NOTE

The database title and database file name are not the same. The database file name is used to identify the file so it can be recognized by the computer and human users. The database title is used on forms and reports as a type of heading, as shown in Figure 2-6.

The Database window displays the database file name.

A form can use the database title as a heading.

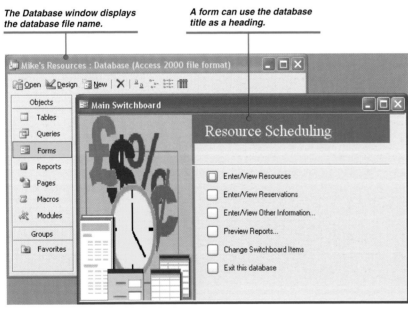

Figure 2-6: The Main Switchboard form displays the title.

Figure 2-7: The Help file presented at the end of the Wizard is more concise than the Access help file.

VIEW YOUR CREATED DATABASE

The final step of the Database Wizard provides options to open that database after it is built and display a help file on using the database. This help file (shown in Figure 2-7) provides basic, yet very useful, information on Access and the objects that make up the database. Make your selections and click **Finish** to watch the building of your database.

The first screen you will see is the Main Switchboard form, as shown in Figure 2-6. Use this form to navigate through the database and accomplish key tasks. This type of form is discussed further in Chapter 6. To view the tables, forms, queries, and reports built for this database, go to the Database window. The Database window is minimized in the lower-left corner of the Access window, as shown in Figure 2-8. Click **Restore** or **Maximize** to display the Database window.

Figure 2-8: The Main Switchboard assists you in accomplishing your tasks while the Database window is minimized.

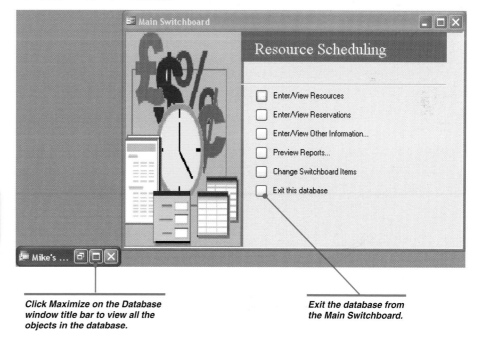

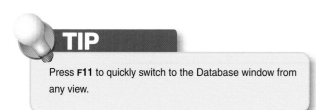

Press **F11** to quickly switch to the Database window from any view.

Click Maximize on the Database window title bar to view all the objects in the database.

Exit the database from the Main Switchboard.

Get Access Samples
from Microsoft's Office Online

A number of database examples can be found at Microsoft's Office web site. You will need an Internet connection.

CHOOSE A SAMPLE DATABASE

1. In Access, click **File | New** and then click **Templates On Office Online** in the New File task pane. This connects you to the Microsoft web site that holds templates for all Office Suite applications. You can also reach this site from the Templates dialog box. See "Jump Ahead Using a Database Template" earlier in the chapter.

2. To find the database examples, verify Templates is displayed in the Search list box at the top of the web page, and type Access in the text box. Click the **Search** arrow and the samples will display, as shown in Figure 2-9.

NOTE

As referenced in Chapter 1, there is a sample database included within Access. You can customize the Northwind sample database just as you can the examples from Office Online. To open this sample, click the Help menu, point at Sample Databases, and select Northwind Sample Database.

Figure 2-9: Microsoft's Office Online holds resources for Access.

Select from multiple pages of database examples.

Business and personal Access database examples are available for download.

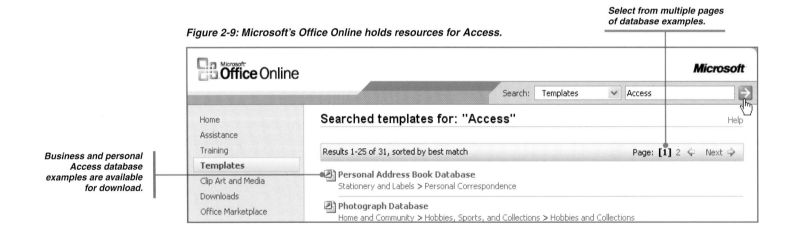

DOWNLOAD THE DATABASE

To save one of the sample databases for your own use, click the database file you want from the list. The next screen, as shown in Figure 2-10, will display an example of your chosen database as well as the download size and lowest version of Access required to run the file. See Chapter 1 for information about opening older version Access files.

This refers to the minimum version of Access required to run the template.

Download times can vary based on speed of Internet connection.

Photograph Database
Home and Community > Hobbies, Sports, and Collections > Hobbies and Collections

Figure 2-10: Sample databases provide great examples that can be customized.

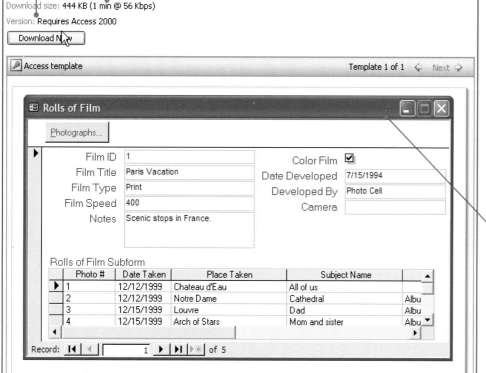

Sample pictures display the "look" of the database without application interactivity.

1. Click **Download Now**, as shown in Figure 2-10. This will lead you to the Template Download page.

2. Click **Download Now** a second time to display the File Download dialog box.

3. Select **Save this File Now**, and click **OK**. You should now see the Save As dialog box.

4. Open the **Save In** box and browse until you find the location where you want the downloaded file saved. Click **Save**. Depending on your Internet connection speed, this may take a couple of minutes. The Download Complete dialog box will confirm the file has been downloaded. Click **Close**.

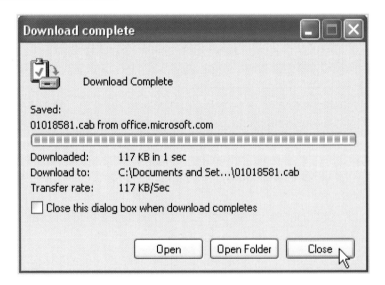

MAKE THE DATABASE USEFUL FOR YOU

Many Access database files save in read-only format when downloaded. To ensure you will be able to make changes to this sample database, you need to remove the read-only format.

1. After downloading the database sample file, go to the location where you saved the file. The downloaded database sample files are usually in the cabinet file (.cab) format. To make the file expand and change to a standard Access database format (.mdb), double-click the file. Your new Access database icon will be displayed. (If you have a third party file compression program installed, such as WinZip, it will open and you can expand the .mdb file from there.)

2. Double-click the database icon to extract the file. You will see the Select A Destination dialog box. Browse to where you would like to save the database, and select the location. Click **Extract**.

3. Go to the file location where you saved the extracted file.

4. Select your database. Open **File**, and click **Properties**. The file's properties dialog box will open.

5. On the General tab, click the **Read-only** box at the bottom of the dialog box to remove the check mark. This will unlock your database, allowing you to modify and add data freely. Click **OK**. This will take you back to your selected database file.

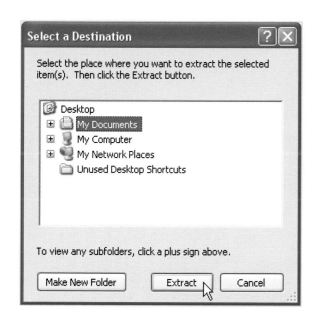

OPEN THE SAMPLE DATABASE

Select **File** and click **Open**. Click **Open** in the Security Warning dialog box if it is displayed. Your sample database will be displayed within Access, as shown in Figure 2-11. These sample files are different from the Access templates on your computer in that they don't use wizards to build sample databases; they are completed databases, ready to be modified or used in their present form. Do one or more of the following:

- Use the Main Switchboard to enter or view information. (See Chapter 4 for information on entering and editing data.)

- Close the Main Switchboard and display the Database window to tour the objects that comprise the sample database. (See Chapter 1 for more information on the Database window.)

- Close the sample database and/or Access.

Build a Database on Your Own

Although the ease with which wizards and samples assist in the creation of databases is undeniable, there is something to be said for working from your own blueprint. Sometimes the templates don't have the solution you are looking for. Sometimes you want to create a more simplistic database to better understand the inner workings of Access. Either way, it is at this point that you will start with a blank database:

1. If the New File task pane isn't displayed, open **File | New**.

2. In the New File task pane, click **Blank Database** at the top of the pane.

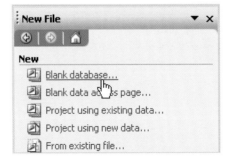

Clicking the Close button will close this form and allow you to view the other objects.

Figure 2-11: Most sample databases greet you with a Main Switchboard form.

Clicking Exit This Database will close the entire database file.

File name:	Morgan's Mopeds
Save as type:	Microsoft Office Access Database

3. The File New Database dialog box will be displayed. Type a file name for your database in the File Name text box, or use the default name. Browse to the folder where you want your new database located. Click **Create**. You will see the Access Database window, as shown in Figure 2-12.

Selected objects show their respective creation methods in the right pane.

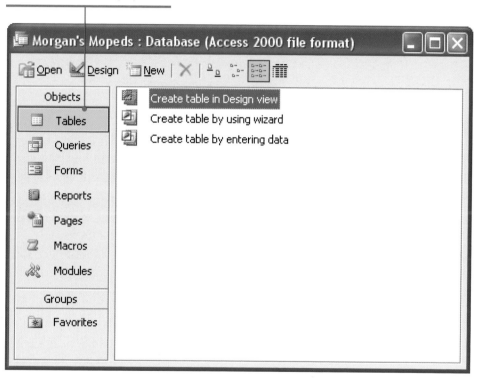

Figure 2-12: The Database window is the Grand Central Station of your database, presenting all objects contained in your database.

Build the Framework with Tables

Although Access is comprised of many objects, the basic database framework revolves around tables. Each table usually holds information about a single topic and is connected or related to other tables through similar pieces of information (or fields). If you are building your own database and have just created a blank database, you will need to develop some tables in which to hold your data. Once again, Access eases the pain of creation by providing a table wizard. If automated tasks are not to your liking, you can choose to create tables manually. The following sections cover both methods.

Start the Table Wizard

The Table Wizard provides some of the most commonly created business and personal tables. You can choose from multiple tables and select individual fields to create your own custom table.

1. Open a blank or existing Access database. See Chapter 1 for ways to open existing databases, or see "Build a Database on Your Own," earlier in this chapter, to see how to create a new one.

2. Open the Database window and select **Tables**.

3. To launch the Table Wizard, either:

   • Double-click **Create Table By Using Wizard**.

   –Or–

   • Click the **New** button, select **Table Wizard** (as shown in Figure 2-13), and click **OK**.

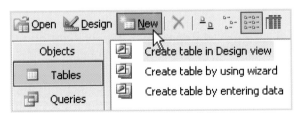

Figure 2-13: New tables can be created in five different ways. The last two items are methods utilizing data from other tables.

CHOOSE THE SAMPLE TABLES AND FIELDS

The first step of the Table Wizard presents over 40 sample fields that can be included in your new table. You can select the entire sample table or simply one field.

1. Click both **Business** and **Personal** option buttons to view the sample tables.

2. Scroll through the **Sample Tables** list, as shown in Figure 2-14, and select the different tables to view the corresponding fields.

3. Select the tables or fields you would like to include in your table. For more information on selecting tables and fields look at the QuickSteps, "Selecting Tables and Fields."

NOTE

It is important to have each table hold a single topic. This provides better structure for relating tables (see relate tables later in this chapter). If there are multiple table samples that would fit your design needs, create separate tables within your own database, and then copy the samples.

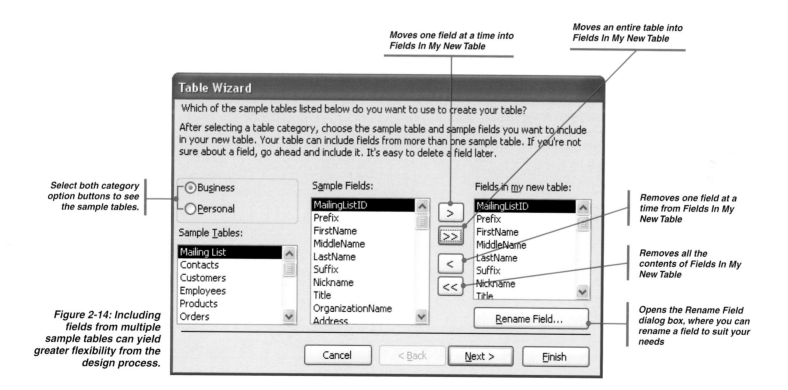

Moves one field at a time into Fields In My New Table

Moves an entire table into Fields In My New Table

Select both category option buttons to see the sample tables.

Removes one field at a time from Fields In My New Table

Removes all the contents of Fields In My New Table

Opens the Rename Field dialog box, where you can rename a field to suit your needs

Figure 2-14: Including fields from multiple sample tables can yield greater flexibility from the design process.

SELECTING TABLES AND FIELDS FROM THE TABLE WIZARD

SELECT TABLES

The first step of the Table Wizard presents over 40 tables from which to choose fields or entire tables. If all the fields in a given table fit with your design criteria, select them all.

1. Select a table from the Sample Tables list box.

2. Click the **double right arrow**. All fields from the chosen sample table will be displayed in the Fields In My New Table list box.

Not satisfied with the results?

3. Click **double left arrow** to remove all the fields, or click **single left arrow** to remove individual fields.

SELECT FIELDS

1. To choose individual fields from the sample tables, select a table from the Sample Tables list box.

2. Choose a field from the Sample Fields list box.

3. Click the **single right arrow** to add a field.

4. To remove a field, click the **single left arrow**.

Continue Steps 1 - 3 until your table holds the necessary fields. Click **Next** to continue with the wizard.

RENAME FIELDS

You may need to rename a field to provide better definition within your own database. For example, you may want to change the title of an address field to "home address."

1. In the first dialog box of the Table Wizard, select the field in the Fields In My New Table list box.

2. Click **Rename Field**. The Rename Field dialog box will be displayed.

3. Type your new field name in the Rename Field box, and click **OK**. The new name will be displayed within the Fields In My New Table list box.

4. Repeat this process as needed, and select **Next** when finished.

NAME THE TABLE AND ESTABLISH A PRIMARY KEY

In the second step of the Table Wizard, you name your table.

1. Type a table name into the What Do You Want To Name Your Table? text box, or accept the wizard's default name, as seen in Figure 2-15.

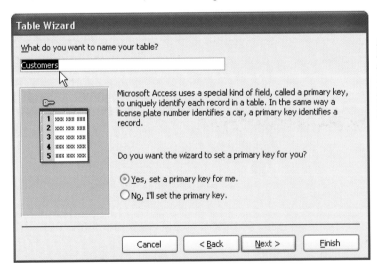

*Figure 2-15:
In the second
step of the
Table Wizard,
you can
create a name
for your table.*

2. Select the primary key yourself or have the Access Wizard do it. Primary keys are fields that uniquely identify records. They ensure duplicate records are not entered and make it faster for the database to locate records. It is through primary keys that databases are connected, or related. Click **Next**.

3. If you choose to select the primary key, after clicking **Next** you will view a dialog box requesting the desired primary key field. Click the **down arrow**, as shown in Figure 2-16, to display all fields available. Select the primary key field. The wizard also presents three options for the type of data the primary key will hold, as shown in Figure 2-16. Select the primary key data type, and click **Next**.

Figure 2-16: Select a primary key field that will hold only unique values.

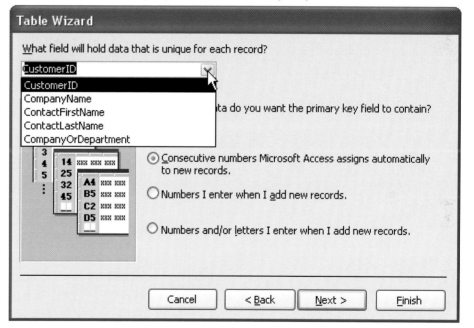

4. If your database currently has other tables residing in it, a dialog box will display providing an opportunity to relate your tables. The wizard usually creates relationships between tables with matching or similar records. (See "Relating Tables" later in this chapter for more information.) Click **Next** to move to the final step of the wizard.

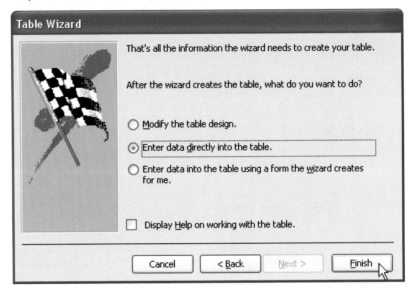

CHOOSE A FINISHED VIEW

In the final step of the Table Wizard, you pick the view you will see after creating the table. Select your view and click **Finish** to create the table.

- Click **Modify The Table Design** to change fields, define properties, or provide additional fields to your table. See Chapter 2 for more information on working with tables in Design view.
- Click **Enter Data Directly Into The Table** to enter data in your new table using Datasheet view.
- Click **Enter Data Into The Table Using A Form** to have Access create a form based on the table you have created.

Create a Table with Data Entry

If you are an active spreadsheet user, it may be more comfortable for you to start using Access by creating a table simply by entering data into the datasheet.

OPEN THE TABLE

1. Open a blank or existing Access database. See Chapter 1 for ways to open existing databases, or see "Build a Database on Your Own," earlier in this chapter, to see how to create a new one.

2. Open the Database window and select **Tables**.

3. To open an empty table (or *datasheet*), as shown in Figure 2-17, either:

   • Double-click **Create Table By Entering Data**.

   –Or–

   • Click the **New** button, select **Datasheet View**, and click **OK**

The column headings, or Field names, can be changed by double clicking them.

Enter data in the cells, or records, as you would in a spreadsheet (see Chapter 4 for information on entering data).

Tab to move between fields.

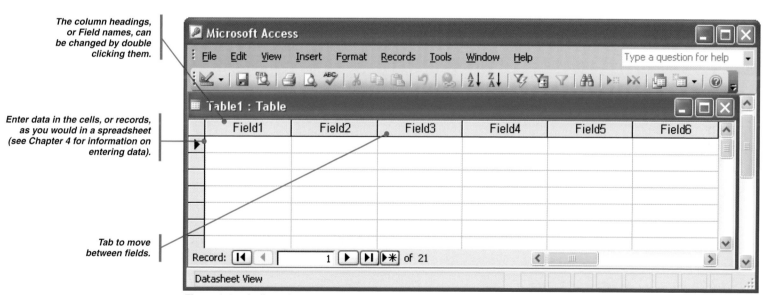

Figure 2-17: At first glance, the Datasheet view of a blank database resembles a spreadsheet.

ENTER DATA

1. Enter data as you would in a spreadsheet. As you move from one row to the next, Access saves that row, or record. See Chapter 4 for additional information on entering and editing data.

2. As shown in Figure 2-17, the column headings are Field 1, Field 2, Field 3, and so forth. Double-click the **Field** names and type your own headings. See Chapter 3 for additional information on modifying field names.

SAVE THE TABLE

1. Click **File | Save**.

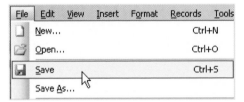

2. Type a name for your table in the Save As dialog box.

3. Click **OK**. A warning dialog box will display, stating that you have no primary key defined for this table. Primary fields are discussed earlier in this chapter. By clicking **Yes** Access will create a primary key for you and add a field using the AutoNumber data type for its content. This means the field or column will automatically generate a unique number for each new row or record you add. After you decide on the primary key, the table will be displayed. See "Create a Primary Key," later in the chapter.

NOTE

When you save the new datasheet, Access analyzes your data and automatically places the most logical data type and format for each field.

Build a Table in Design View

Tables can be created manually, adding fields one at a time. To use this method you must start in Design view.

OPEN THE TABLE

1. Open a blank or existing Access database. See Chapter 1 for ways to open existing databases, or see "Build a Database on Your Own," earlier in this chapter, to see how to create a new one.

2. To open a blank table in Design view, either:

   ● Double-click **Create Table In Design View**.

   –Or–

   ● Click the **New** button, select **Design View**, and click **OK**.

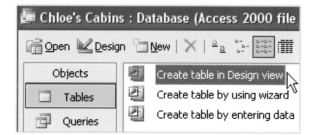

CREATE THE FIELD STRUCTURE

As shown in Figure 2-18, the upper section of the table design window has columns which hold the basic field definitions for each field included in your table. The field name, data type, and description for each individual field are entered into the rows. The lower portion of this window is where you set more specific field properties, which is discussed in more detail in Chapter 3. This section changes as you select different fields.

Field Names describe characteristics of your database topic.

Data Types refer to the type of data entered into the field and can be made up of 10 different types.

Descriptions ensure that others will understand appropriate data entry.

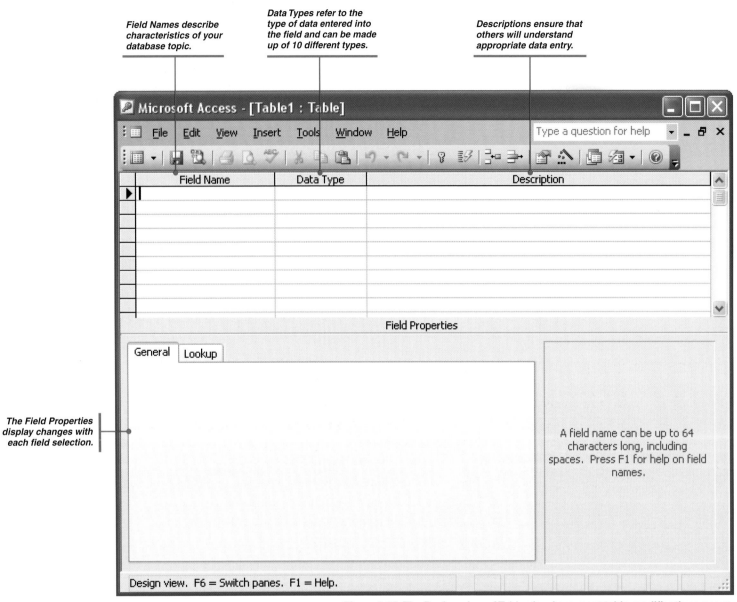

The Field Properties display changes with each field selection.

Figure 2-18: The Design view of Tables is where most table modifications occur.

Data Type defines the type of data the field will contain. See Table 2-1 for the different data types and their usage. Text is the default data type, as it provides the most flexibility with data entry.

TABLE 2-1: DATA TYPES YOU CAN ASSIGN TO AN ACCESS FIELD

DATA TYPE	DESCRIPTION
Text	Numbers or letters, up to 255 characters
Memo	Text usually too long to be stored in text, up to 65,535 characters
Number	Only digits
Date/Time	A valid date
Currency	Same as number, but with decimal places and currency symbol
AutoNumber	A unique sequential number
Yes/No	Accepts yes/no, true/false, on/off
OLE Object	Any object that can be linked or embedded in a table
Hyperlink	A path to an object, file or web site
Lookup Wizard	Creates a drop-down list from an existing list or one you create

1. Place insertion point in the first row of the Field Name column and type a field name.

2. Press the **TAB** key. This will move your cursor to the Data Type column.

3. Click the **down arrow** to open the Data Type drop-down menu, as shown in Figure 2-19.

4. Select a data type. Press **TAB** to move to the Description column.

5. Enter a description for your field.

6. Press **TAB** or **ENTER**, or use your mouse to move to the next field or row.

7. Repeat Steps 2 - 6 until you have entered all of the field descriptions for the table.

TIP

Be sure to enter a description for each field in the Description column of Design view, as these descriptions are displayed in the datasheet's status bar when the field is selected. Meaningful descriptions can greatly assist other users when entering data.

Employees : Table				
Employee ID	Department Name	First Name	Last Name	Title
1	Management	Dana	Phillip	CIO
2	Management	Lyle	Bryant	CEO
3	Production	Morgan	Danae	Inspector
4	Production	Chloe	Faith	Inspector
5	Legal	Michael	Edward	Attorney
6	Human Resources	Sherelen	Gail	HR Director
7	Advertising	Dorothy	Jewel	Sales Manag
(AutoNumber)				

Record: 1 of 7

Name of Department: Management, Advertising, Production, Legal or Human Resources

ASSIGNING A PRIMARY KEY

On occasion, your table may be without a primary key or has the primary key in the wrong field.

INSERT A PRIMARY KEY INTO A "KEYLESS" TABLE

1. In the Database window, select the keyless table. Click Open on the Database window toolbar. You should see the file in datasheet view.
2. Click **View | Design View**.

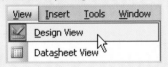

3. Click the far-left column, or *row selector*, of the chosen primary key field. The row should be highlighted, identified by a right pointing triangle.
4. Click the **Primary Key** button on the Table Design toolbar.

CHANGE PRIMARY KEY FIELDS

1. Open the table.
2. Select the old primary key field by clicking the **Primary Key** icon within the far-left, or row selector, column.
3. Click the Primary Key button on the Table Design toolbar. There should no longer be a key next to the old primary key field name.
4. Select the new primary key field by placing the insertion point anywhere in the field's row.
5. Click the **Primary Key** button on the toolbar. You will see a small key appear in the far-left column next to the primary key field name.

Figure 2-19: Text is the default data type for all field entries.

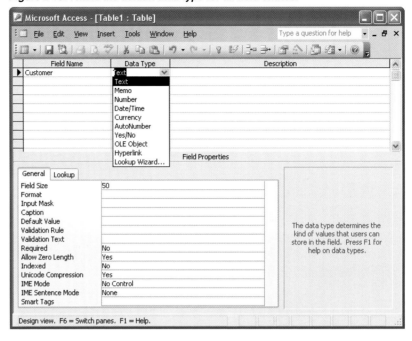

CREATE A PRIMARY KEY

It is important to assign one field as a primary key. Primary keys are fields that identify records as unique. They ensure duplicate records are not entered and expedite location of records in the database. It is also through primary keys that databases are connected, or related.

1. Select the field or multiple fields that are appropriate primary keys by clicking any part of the row with the chosen field.
2. Click **Edit | Primary Key**. A key will appear in the far left column of the selected field.

SAVE THE TABLE DESIGN

After entering all of your field definitions, save the table design by naming it.

1. Click **File | Save**.

2. Enter the name for your table, and click **OK**. Your table will be displayed in Design view.

Add Identifying Information

You can add identifying information to an Access database to make it easier to find.

1. Open your database file using one of the methods discussed in Chapter 1.

2. Open **File** and select **Properties**.

3. Type identifying information, as shown in Figure 2-20. Good descriptors would include a title, subject, and keywords (words or phrases that are associated with the database).

Figure 2-20: The search for a particular database can be eased by entering identifying data.

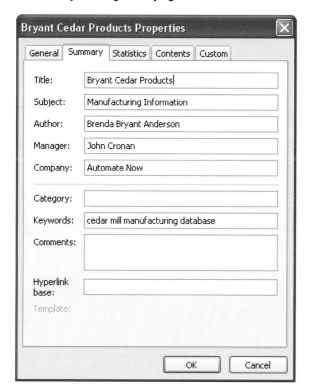

Identify Relationships

Access is a *relational* database: it uses relationships to establish connections between tables. Each table, or group of data, should have a primary key, and that primary key can also be part of another table but viewed as a *foreign key*. Because this same primary key is in both tables, the two tables can relate and mix in multiple settings—such as queries, forms, reports and data access pages.

Define Relationships

Table relationships are defined as one-to-many and many-to-many. This is because some tables hold a single record that relates to multiple records in another database. For example, a small moped manufacturer has a database with three tables. The tables are as shown in Figure 2-21. The Orders table can hold many orders from the same customer. This would be a one-to-many

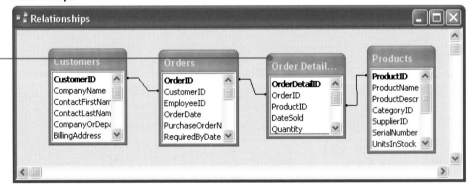

Figure 2-21: Different relationships can be established among the three tables.

relationship. Each order can have multiple products on it and, reversing the thought, each product can be on multiple orders. This would be a many-to-many relationship.

The ideal way to relate the latter relationship is to create a third *junction*, or linking table (shown as Order Details in Figure 2-22).

Figure 2-22: Junction tables create the connection between tables having a many-to-many relationship.

Here, the Order Details table acts as the junction table.

Relate Tables

Access has an easy way to relate tables, once you've defined their similar primary keys.

1. Close all tables and open the Database window.

2. To display the Show Tables dialog box, either:

- Click the **Relationships** button on the toolbar.

  –Or–

- Click **Tools | Relationships**.

3. Select a table and click **Add**. Repeat to add all the tables needed to create relationships.

4. Click **Close**. The Relationships window will be displayed. The primary key fields are the bold typeface fields within each table list.

5. Drag the primary key field from one table to the equivalent foreign key field in another table, as shown in Figure 2-23. Continue dragging the primary key fields until all chosen tables are related.

6. Close the Relationships dialog box.

7. Click **Yes** if asked to save changes to the relationships layout.

Figure 2-23: Two records are joined by the primary key.

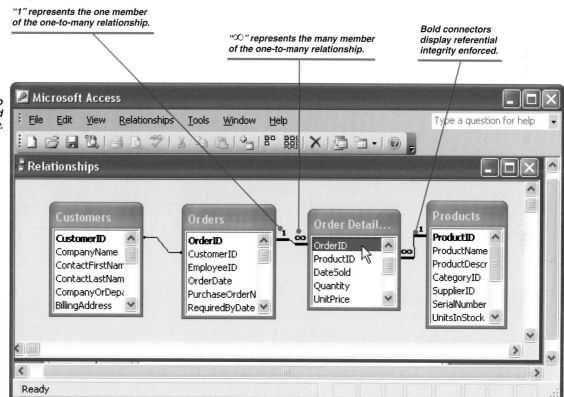

"1" represents the one member of the one-to-many relationship.

"∞" represents the many member of the one-to-many relationship.

Bold connectors display referential integrity enforced.

Enforce Referential Integrity

Referential Integrity allows Access to check the validity of relationships between records. It also ensures that changes, such as deleting or altering related data, don't impair the relationships.

1. Click the **Relationships** button on the Database window to view the relationships between the tables in your database.

2. Double-click the line representing the relationship that you want to apply referential integrity to.

3. At the bottom of the Edit Relationships dialog box, select **Enforce Referential Integrity**, as shown in Figure 2-24.

4. Choose:

   - Select **Cascade Update Related Fields** to ensure changing a primary key value in the primary table automatically updates the foreign key field.

   - Select **Cascade Delete Related Records** to ensure when records are deleted in the primary table corresponding records in a related table will also be deleted.

5. Click **OK**. Close the Relationships window.

6. If prompted, select **Yes** to save changes to the relationships layout.

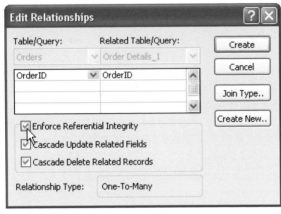

NOTE

You have to select Enforce Referential Integrity to have the option of implementing Cascade Update Related Fields or Cascade Delete Related Records made available.

Figure 2-24: Enforcing referential integrity ensures that any change you might make will not impair the relationships established in your tables.

How to...

- *Delete a Table*
- *Rename a Table*
- *Change Field Names*
- *Switching Views*
- *Choose a Data Type*
- *Change Display of Data Through the Format Property*
- *Create a Pattern for Data Entry with Input Masks*
- *Editing and Entering Input Masks*
- *Establish a Field's Default Value*
- *Limit Field Values with a Validation Rule*
- *Require Entry but Allow a Zero Length String*
- *Use the Caption Field Property*
- *Index a Data Field*
- *Add Smart Tags*
- *Use the Lookup Wizard*
- *View a Subdatasheet*
- *Create a Subdatasheet*

Chapter 3

Modifying Tables and Fields

As with any powerful machine, an Access database requires some fine-tuning to optimize its purpose and performance. The modifications covered in this chapter involve table changes and field adjustments to the field properties. Basic table changes will occur within the Database window, as shown in Figure 3-1. Field adjustments will happen later in the chapter, and you will work with the field properties area of the table Design view.

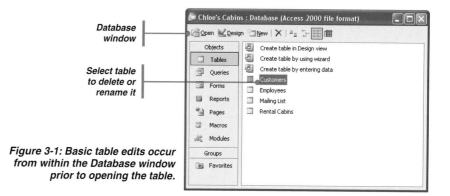

Figure 3-1: Basic table edits occur from within the Database window prior to opening the table.

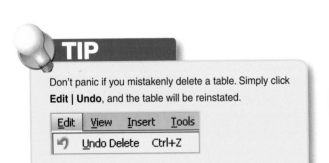

NOTE

In order to make changes within a table or any object in a database, the database file must not be in read-only format. To check this attribute, first ensure that your database file is closed. Next, locate and select your database file in Windows Explorer. Click **File | Properties** and select the **General** tab. At the bottom of the dialog box in the Attributes area, ensure that the Read-Only check box is deselected.
Click **OK**
when finished. Now you can open your file and make modifications.

Attributes: ☐ Read-only ☐ Hidden

TIP

Don't panic if you mistakenly delete a table. Simply click **Edit | Undo**, and the table will be reinstated.

| Edit | View | Insert | Tools |
| ↶ | Undo Delete | Ctrl+Z | |

Make Basic Changes to Tables and Fields

Tables and their fields often need to be adapted. This is an easy task within Microsoft Access.

Delete a Table

When a table is no longer necessary, you can easily delete it.

1. Within the Database window, select the **Tables** object, as shown in Figure 3-1.

2. Select the table you want deleted.

3. Press the **DELETE** key. A dialog box will be displayed. Click **Yes** to confirm the deletion. This will bring you back to the Database window. (If you have established relationships between tables, continue to Step 4.)

Microsoft Office Access

⚠ **Do you want to delete the table 'Mailing List'?**

For more information on how to prevent this message from displaying every time you delete an object, click Help.

[Yes] [No] [Help]

4. If you have established relationships between the table you want deleted and other tables, you will see another alert dialog box. See Chapter 2 for information regarding table relationships. The alert informs you of the need to delete the relationships with this table prior to its deletion. It also offers to delete the relationships for you. Click **Yes** if you would like to delete both the relationships and the table. This will bring you back to the Database window.

Microsoft Office Access

⚠ **You can't delete the table 'Schedule' until its relationships to other tables have been deleted.**

Do you want Microsoft Office Access to delete the relationships now?

[Yes] [No]

Rename a Table

Changing the name of a table is a simple task, if you are at the right location.

1. In order to rename a table, you must have the table closed and be in the Database window, as shown in Figure 3-1.

2. Click the table within the Database window. Then either:

   ● Click **Edit | Rename**.

   –Or–

   ● Pause for a moment, and click the table a second time.

   There will now be a border around the table name, and its contents will be highlighted.

Edit	View	Insert	Tools
Can't Undo			Ctrl+Z
Cut			Ctrl+X
Copy			Ctrl+C
Office Clipboard...			
Paste			Ctrl+V
Delete			Del
Rename			F2

3. Type the new table name, and press **ENTER**. The new table name will be displayed within the Database window. `Customers`

Change Field Names

Later in this chapter, we will go into Table Design view and change field properties. To change a field name, however, you may follow a similar path as above in "Rename a Table."

1. In the Database window, double-click the table with the field name you want to change. The table will open.

2. Double-click the field name you want to change.

	Field Name	Data Type
🔑	EmployeeID	AutoNumber
	DepartmentName	Text
	SocialSecurityNumber	Text
▶	EmployeeNumber	Text
	NationalEmplNumber	Text
	FirstName	Text
	MiddleName	Text

3. Type a new name and press **ENTER** to accept the new field name and save the table.

To quickly enter a data type in the data type column of design view, just type its first letter when the data type cell is active.

Fine Tune the Fields

The fine-tuning that can take place within fields and their properties is quite extensive. The first part of this tuning revolves around the field's data type. As presented in "Build a Table in Design View," in Chapter 2, there are ten data types to choose from when first defining a field. This section takes you a step deeper into not only the data types, as shown in Figure 3-2, but also the properties that further define those data types.

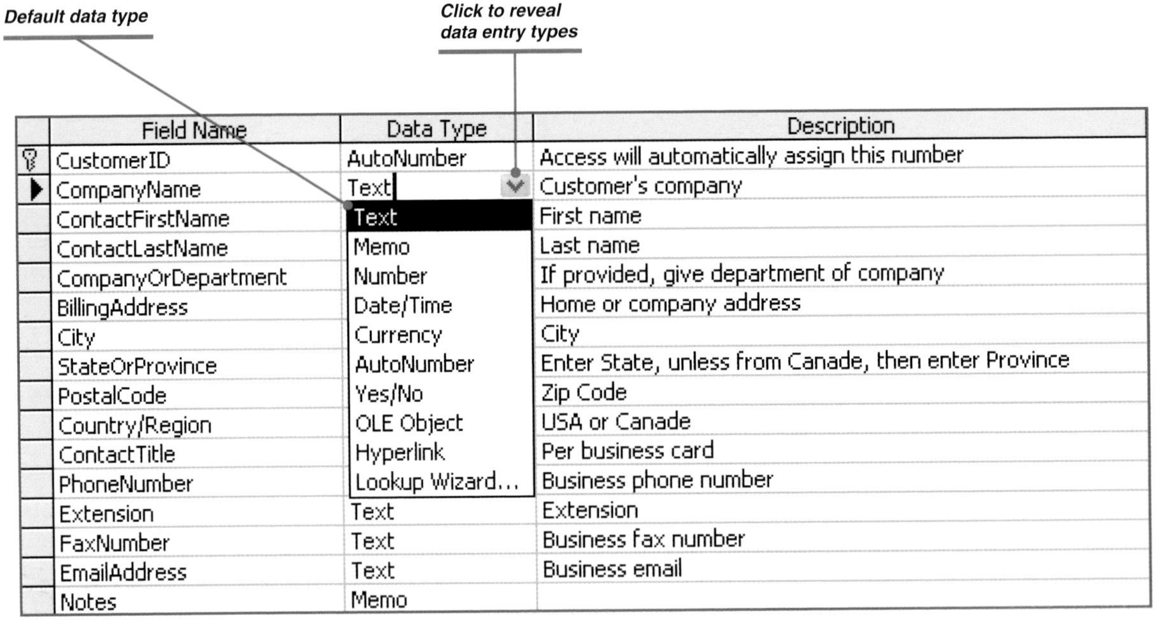

Default data type

Click to reveal
data entry types

	Field Name	Data Type	Description
	CustomerID	AutoNumber	Access will automatically assign this number
▶	CompanyName	Text	Customer's company
	ContactFirstName	Text	First name
	ContactLastName	Memo	Last name
	CompanyOrDepartment	Number	If provided, give department of company
	BillingAddress	Date/Time	Home or company address
	City	Currency	City
	StateOrProvince	AutoNumber	Enter State, unless from Canade, then enter Province
	PostalCode	Yes/No	Zip Code
	Country/Region	OLE Object	USA or Canade
	ContactTitle	Hyperlink	Per business card
	PhoneNumber	Lookup Wizard...	Business phone number
	Extension	Text	Extension
	FaxNumber	Text	Business fax number
	EmailAddress	Text	Business email
	Notes	Memo	

Figure 3-2: Ten data types allow you to restrict what data is entered in a field.

SWITCHING VIEWS

When editing tables and the fields within those tables, you will be switching between Datasheet view and Design view frequently. There are a few ways to switch views. Find the way that is quickest for you.

SWITCH VIEWS WITH THE TOOLBAR VIEW BUTTON

Click the **View** button to toggle between Datasheet view and Design view. The picture within the button indicates the view that will be displayed when clicked. Remember, the icon within the button is not the view you are currently in; it is the view you will go to when the button is clicked.

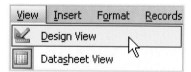

SWITCH VIEWS WITH THE TOOLBAR -VIEW DOWN ARROW

1. Click the **View down arrow** to display a list of the available views. See Chapter 10 for information regarding PivotTable and PivotChart views.

2. Scroll down and click to select a different view.

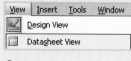

SWITCH VIEWS WITH THE VIEW MENU

- Click **View**. Then click **Datasheet View** or **Design View**, depending on what you want to display.

—Or—

- Press **ALT+V** to open the View menu from the keyboard. Press **D** for Design view, or press **S** for Datasheet view.

Choose a Data Type

The data types can restrict certain information from being entered incorrectly into the database. For example, if a number is entered into a field and a user tries to enter text, a warning dialog box will appear; Access will not accept the entry until a number is supplied. All fine-tuning of the database, including data type definition, begins in the Database window.

1. In the Database window, select the table to be customized. Click **Open** on the Database window toolbar. You should see the file in Datasheet view.

2. Change to Design view by clicking **View | Design View**. (See the Quicksteps, "Switching Views," for other methods of switching views.)

3. Click the Data Type down arrow next to the field name you want to fine tune.

4. Select the **Data Type**, as shown in Figure 3-2.

Change Display of Data Through the Format Property

The Field Properties area of the Table Design view, as shown in Figure 3-3, presents numerous ways to customize your table and restrict the type of data being entered.

Lists properties for the current field

Displays description of selected cell

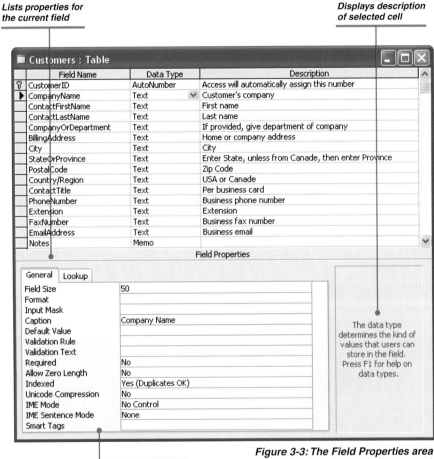

Figure 3-3: The Field Properties area within Design view provides several ways to fine tune the fields.

Field properties will change depending on the selected data type.

NOTE

There is a difference between a *selected* field and a field that has been made *active*. When *selecting* a field, you click the row selector when the mouse pointer is a rightward pointing arrow, and the whole row becomes highlighted. A field is *active* when the right triangle is displayed in its row selector. To edit the field properties of a field, the field must be made active, but it need not be selected.

WORK WITH FORMAT SYMBOLS

You can change the way data is displayed (not stored) in a database by entering specific symbols into the Format text box of the Field Properties area. Several symbols are used within the Format text box, many unique to one or two data types. The symbols used in the Text data type are listed in Table 3-1.

TABLE 3-1: TEXT DATA TYPE FORMAT SYMBOLS

SYMBOL	DISPLAY PURPOSE:
>	Uppercase characters
<	Lowercase characters
@	Placeholder for character or space (Placeholders fill underlying data from right to left.)
&	Placeholder for character or optional space
!	Left aligns data and forces placeholders to fill from left to right; must be first character in format string
"Text"	Displays item in quotation marks exactly as typed, in addition to data
\	Displays a character immediately following data
*	Fills all blank spaces with character following *
[color]	Formats data text in black, blue, green, cyan, red, magenta, yellow, or white; must be used with other symbols

DISPLAY ALL CHARACTERS IN UPPERCASE

You can format a field to display its contents in uppercase letters. For example, if you have a State field, you could ensure all two-letter abbreviations, such as WA, are uppercased.

1. Open the table in Design view.

2. Click the field you want formatted. A right-facing triangle will display in the row selector to confirm the field is active, as shown in Figure 3-4.

3. Click the **General** tab in the Field Properties area.

4. Click the **Format** text box and type > (or to accomplish another formatting task, choose the appropriate symbol, as shown in Table 3-1). If you have additional objects within the database, the **AutoCorrect Options** button will display to the left of the text box.

5. Click the **AutoCorrect Options** button, and select **Update Format Everywhere *Fieldname* is Used** from the menu.

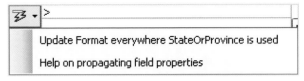

By doing so, the format you have chosen will be propagated across all objects with the selected field name. For example, if you formatted the state field to uppercase, all state fields—whether in forms, queries, reports or other tables—will be changed to uppercase. If no objects contain the same field name as your newly formatted field, a dialog box will display a message stating that no objects needed to be updated. Click **OK**.

6. In order to view your changes, you must save the table. If you try to switch views prior to saving, a dialog box will appear requesting you first save the table. Click **Yes** to save changes, and the display will switch to Datasheet view.

Click the field to be formatted

Figure 3-4: Format a field to display and print uppercase letters by using the ">" symbol.

Field Name	Data Type	Descriptio
▶ StateOrProvince	Text	State of Billing Address
PostalCode	Text	Zip Code
Country/Region	Text	Country
Businessphone	Text	Business number
Homephone	Text	Home number
EmailAddress	Text	Business email address
Notes	Memo	
Website	Hyperlink	

Field Properties

General Lookup

Field Size	20
Format	>
Input Mask	
Caption	State/Province

Click down arrow to see previously used format symbols

Create a Pattern for Data Entry with Input Masks

Input masks provide a pattern for formatting data within a field by using characters or symbols to control how data will be displayed. There are actually three parts to an input mask. The first part includes the mask characters or mask *string* (series of characters) along with embedded literal data—such as parentheses, periods, and hyphens. The second part is optional and refers to the embedded literal characters and their storage within the field. If the second part is set at "0," it will store the characters; "1" means the characters will only be displayed, not stored. The third part of the string indicates the single character used as a placeholder. An example of a telephone number input mask would be: **!\(999")"000\-0000;0;_.**

- Exclamation point (!) indicates the mask should fill data from right to left.
- Backslash (\) causes characters immediately following to be displayed as a literal character. In this case, the parenthesis is the literal character.
- "9" character means optional digits can be entered into these spaces.
- Double quotation ("") is like the backslash in that anything enclosed in this will be taken literally.
- "0" characters means a single digit is mandatory.

An example of the displayed phone number would be (555)555-1212. Table 3-2 provides more detailed descriptions of mask characters. However, Access provides an easier way to enter input masks than to create one from scratch. The Input Mask Wizard is a simple tool to use.

1. Open a table in Design view.
2. Click the field you want to have an input mask.
3. Click the **General** tab in the Field Properties area.
4. Click anywhere inside the Input Mask text box. You will see a Build button at the right side of the text box. Click the **Build** button to display the Input Mask Wizard.
5. In the Input Mask drop-down list, click the mask you want to use as shown in Figure 3-5. (Click **Try It** to enter data and see how it will be displayed.) If no changes are needed, click **Next** and proceed to step 7.

QUICKSTEPS

EDITING AND ENTERING INPUT MASKS

The Input Mask Wizard provides great sample patterns for some of the most common formatting situations. However, you may want to customize one of the patterns to use a format specific to your circumstance. There are two methods for doing this. The first is within the Input Mask Wizard and the second is directly in the Input Mask text box.

EDIT INPUT MASKS WITH INPUT MASK WIZARD

1. Open your database in Design view and click the field you would like to format with an input mask.

2. Click the **Build** button (at the right of the Input Mask Caption text box) to start the Input Mask Wizard.

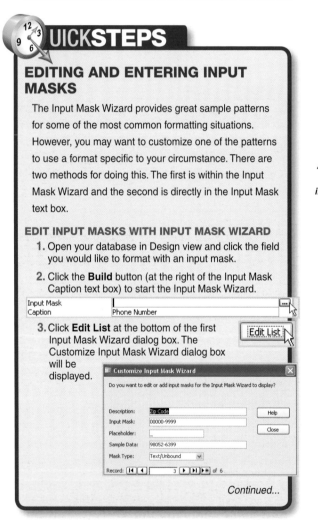

3. Click **Edit List** at the bottom of the first Input Mask Wizard dialog box. The Customize Input Mask Wizard dialog box will be displayed.

Continued...

Figure 3-5: Input masks assist in formatting common data types.

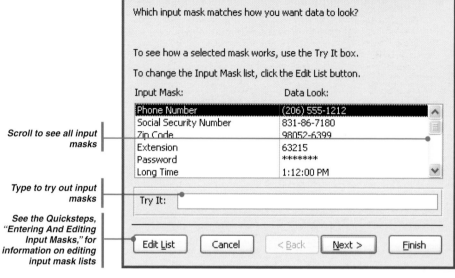

Scroll to see all input masks

Type to try out input masks

See the Quicksteps, "Entering And Editing Input Masks," for information on editing input mask lists

6. If changes in the input mask are needed, type them into the Input Mask text box. You will also see in Figure 3-6 an area that allows you to change the default placeholder. Either keep the default or click the **down arrow** at the right side of the text box to open a drop-down menu of placeholders from which to choose. Click **Next** to proceed to the next step.

7. Choose whether to store your data **With The Symbols In The Mask** or **Without The Symbols In The Mask**. (Although choosing to store data with symbols allows them to be displayed in all objects, this method makes the size of your database slightly larger.) Click **Finish** to return to Table Design view.

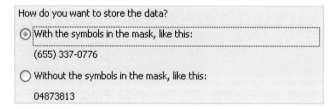

EDITING AND ENTERING INPUT MASKS *(Continued)*

4. Move through the sample input mask records as you would a datasheet (see Chapter 4 for information on working in datasheets). If you see a sample you would like to permanently change, edit the mask by changing the description, input mask symbols, and/or the placeholders. Click **Close** to return to the Input Mask Wizard dialog box.

ENTER INPUT MASKS WITH INPUT MASK WIZARD

1. Open your database in Design view and click the field you would like to format with an input mask.

2. Click the **Build** button (at the right of the Input Mask text box) to start the Input Mask Wizard.

3. Click **Edit List** at the bottom of the first Input Mask Wizard dialog box. The Customize Input Mask Wizard dialog box will be displayed.

4. Click the **New Record** button. ▶✳

5. Type a new description in the Description text box. Press **TAB** to move to the Input Mask text box.

6. Type a new input mask based on the symbols listed in Table 3-2. Press **TAB** and type a placeholder symbol, as displayed in Figure 3-6, in the Placeholder text box. Press **TAB**. In the Sample Text box, type an example and then click **Close**. The Input Mask Wizard dialog box is displayed and your new input mask is listed within the sample list.

EDIT OR ENTER INPUT MASK DIRECTLY IN THE INPUT MASK TEXT BOX

To manually edit or enter an input mask, simply click the Input Mask text box in the Field Properties area. Type your new mask based on the symbols found in Table 3-2.

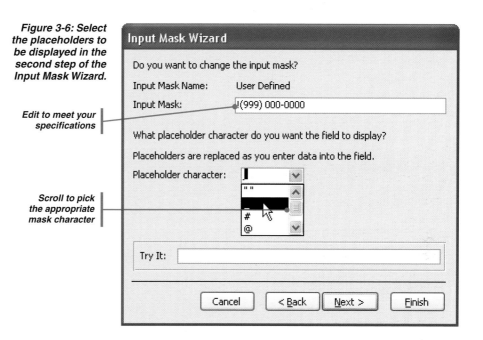

Figure 3-6: Select the placeholders to be displayed in the second step of the Input Mask Wizard.

Input Mask Wizard

Do you want to change the input mask?

Input Mask Name: User Defined

Input Mask: !(999) 000-0000

Edit to meet your specifications

What placeholder character do you want the field to display?

Placeholders are replaced as you enter data into the field.

Placeholder character:

Scroll to pick the appropriate mask character

Try It:

Cancel   < Back   Next >   Finish

TABLE 3-2: INPUT MASK DEFINITION CHARACTERS

MASK CHARACTER:	MEANING:
0	Required single digit (0 to 9)
9	Optional digit (0 to 9)
#	A digit, a space, the plus sign, and the minus sign can be entered
L	Required letter
?	Optional letter
>	Converts all letters that follow to uppercase
<	Converts all letters that follow to lowercase
A	Required digit or letter
a	Optional digit or letter
&	Required character or space
C	Optional character or space
!	Mask will fill from right to left
\	Characters immediately following will be displayed literally
""	Characters enclosed in double quotation will be displayed literally

Establish a Field's Default Value

In many cases, a field contained in multiple records will include the same data. For example, employees of a small company may all reside in the same state. Rather than entering that state several times, place a default value for the state name in field properties.

1. Open a table in Design view.

2. Click the field you want to have a default value.

3. Click the **General** tab in the Field Properties area.

4. Type a value in the Default Value text box, and press **ENTER**. The typed value will automatically become enclosed in double quotes.

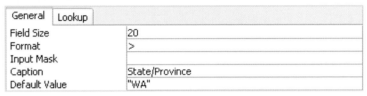

General	Lookup	
Field Size		20
Format		>
Input Mask		
Caption		State/Province
Default Value		"WA"

5. Click **Save** on the Table Design toolbar, and switch to Datasheet view to see how the default value has affected your table.

Limit Field Values with a Validation Rule

Validation rules set parameters around the values inputted. Access applies these validity checks during data entry. A validation rule is made up of an *expression* (a group of functions, characters, and field values) that defines the acceptable values. The expression may be entered manually, or you can use a tool called Expression Builder. Not a wizard, Expression Builder is more of an organizational tool that helps you see the fields you can use and the operators or functions that are available. Chapter 5 provides more detail on using Expression Builder. You can, and should, include some validation text with your validation rule. This text will be displayed in a dialog box if the rule is violated. For example, let's say you have an employee table that holds a "gender" field.

It is designed to have either "M" for male or "F" for female. If a character other than "M" or "F" is entered into the field, the validation text will pop up in a dialog box.

1. Open a table in Design view.

2. Click the field you want to receive a validation rule and validation text.

3. Click the **General** tab in the Field Properties area.

4. Type your rule or expression in the Validation Rule text box, as shown in Figure 3-7. Press **TAB** or **ENTER**. The insertion point will move to the Validation Text text box.

5. Type your validation text and press **ENTER**.

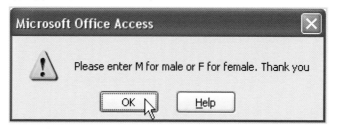

Figure 3-7: Validation rules should also include validation text to assist in data entry.

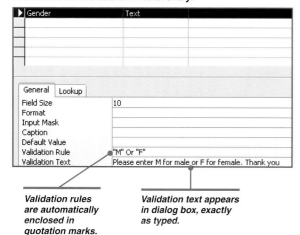

Validation rules are automatically enclosed in quotation marks.

Validation text appears in dialog box, exactly as typed.

6. Click **Save** and select **Datasheet View** to experiment with data entry in the field with validation rules and text. If you don't adhere to the rule you established, Access will alert you with a dialog box and prevent you from making the illegal entry.

Require Entry but Allow a Zero Length String

For certain fields within your database, you may want to require data entry in order to maintain integrity within your database structure.

There are situations where an entry is important, but there is no data to place in the field(s). For example, in a customer table you may choose to require entry of the customers' fax numbers in order to send reservation confirmations. Some customers, however, may not have a fax machine. You would want to require the entry but allow a *zero length string*. This way a blank space, or double apostrophes (" ") could be entered into the fax number field confirming the customer has no fax number.

TIP

You can change field properties by following the same method used to enter new ones. If you would like to delete a previously set property, simply go to the field property text box, select the entry by dragging the mouse over it, and press **DELETE**. Some changes will elicit a warning from Access when you save the table, yet the warning is accompanied by an offer to check the new rule or requirement. If current data doesn't work with the new field property, you will be notified and given the option to revert to the old setting.

1. Open a table in Design view.

2. Click the field you would like to have as required entry.

3. Click the **General** tab in the Field Properties area.

4. In the Required text box, either:

   - Type **Y** for yes, or **N** for no.

   –Or–

   - Click the **Required down arrow** at the right of the text box, and select **Yes** or **No**.

5. Press **TAB** to move to the Allow Zero Length text box. Type <u>Yes</u> or <u>No</u> in the text box using the same techniques as in the required field text box.

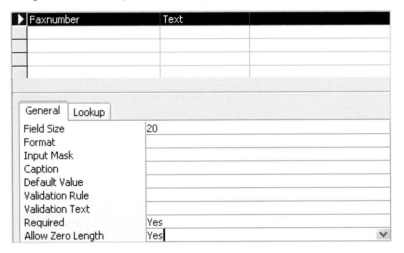

6. Click **Save** and select **Datasheet View** to experiment with required fields. If you don't type data in the required field, Access will alert you with a dialog box and prevent you from entering the record.

Use the Caption Field Property

You may have noticed many of the wizard-based data fields have names with no embedded spaces. For example, rather than "Home Phone," the field name is "HomePhone." If you foresee growth in your database and the potential for upsizing it to a SQL-based database, it is a good idea to follow this practice. SQL databases, such as Oracle or Microsoft SQL Server, do not support spaces within names. To ensure "friendly" names are displayed within your database, however, use the Caption Field Property. This will display your field names with embedded spaces.

1. Open a table in Design view.

2. Click the field name you would like to provide with a "friendly" name.

3. Click the **General** tab in the Field Properties area.

4. Enter your "friendly" name for the field in the Caption text box. As with other field property changes, you must select **Save** prior to switching to Datasheet view.

Index a Data Field

An *index* is an internal table that contains two columns. One holds the value in the field or fields being indexed, and the other holds the physical location of each record in the table containing that value. Access uses an index in a manner similar to how you use a book index: it finds the value desired and jumps directly to the page, or place, where that value is held. Each time a record is added to or updated in the database, Access updates all of its indexes. This may sometimes slow the process of data entry, so overuse of indexes is not recommended.

1. Open a table in Design view.

2. Click the field you want to have indexed.

3. Click the **General** tab in the Field Properties area.

4. Click the **down arrow** at the right of the Indexed text box.

5. "No" is the default choice within the Indexed field. Click **Yes (Duplicates OK)** if the field will have multiple entries with the same value.

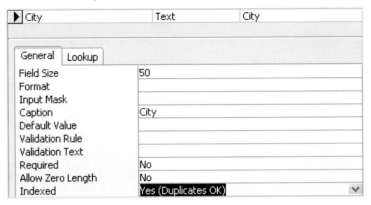

Add Smart Tags

Smart tags are like hyperlinks on steroids. They are little applications you can hook into fields to recognize items—such as names, addresses, or stock symbols—and provide options, or actions, for those recognized items. This is a new feature for Access 2003 and, as such, is limited in the number of Smart tags available within the standard Access application. There is, however, a button within the Smart Tags dialog box, as shown in Figure 3-8, to connect you to the Office Online web site and let you check out current offerings within the Smart tag product line. The current Smart tags included with Access are:

- **Date**, used to schedule a meeting or check your calendar within Microsoft Outlook

- **Financial Symbol**, used to obtain a stock quote, company reports, or news surrounding an accepted NYSE or NASDAQ company—all from the MSN MoneyCentral web site

- **Person Name**, used to accept a person's name or e-mail address, and assuming you are using Microsoft Outlook, send an e-mail, schedule a meeting, open your contact list, or add the name to your contact list

When a Smart tag is added to your field, a drop-down menu will be displayed as your cursor hovers over the field within the record. This menu will provide the above listed Smart tag options.

NOTE

If you would like to hide Smart tags on your datasheet, click **Tools | Options**. Select the Datasheet tab and click to deselect the **Show Smart Tags On Datasheets** check box. Click **OK**.

1. Open a table in Design view.

2. Click the field you would like to include a Smart tag.

3. Click the **General** tab in the Field Properties area.

4. Click the **Build** button to the right of the Smart tags text box. The Smart Tags dialog box will be displayed.

5. Select any of the Smart tags that apply to your field. As you select the smart tag, it will become checked and a description will be displayed in the smart tag detail area of the dialog box, as shown in Figure 3-8.

6. Click **OK** to return to the Design view. Select **Save** and switch to Datasheet view to experiment with Smart tags.

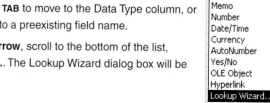

Select one or more
Smart tags

Figure 3-8: Accomplish common tasks by using Smart tags.

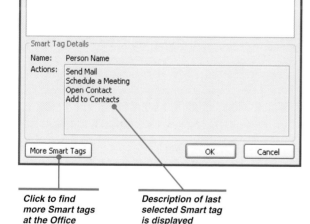

Click to find
more Smart tags
at the Office
Online web site

Description of last
selected Smart tag
is displayed

Use the Lookup Wizard

There are times when the data to be entered in a field can be found in another table and/or the data is a series of data points that would benefit from being provided only once to eliminate data entry errors. Rather than selecting a data type for your field, it may be helpful to call upon the Lookup Wizard to create a drop-down list of values from which you can choose.

START THE LOOKUP WIZARD

1. Open a table in Design view.

2. Type a field name and press **TAB** to move to the Data Type column, or click the data type field next to a preexisting field name.

3. Click the **Data Type down arrow**, scroll to the bottom of the list, and select **Lookup Wizard…**. The Lookup Wizard dialog box will be displayed.

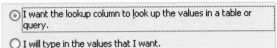

4. Do either:

- Click **I Want The Lookup Column To Look Up The Values In A Table Or Query** to pull data from an existing table or query. Select **Next** and continue through the next section.

- Click **I Will Type In The Values That I Want** if you would like to create your own data list. Select **Next**, and skip to "Create Your Own Value List with the Lookup Wizard."

FIND YOUR LOOKUP VALUES IN A TABLE OR QUERY

1. Use steps 1-3 of "Start the Lookup Wizard."

2. Click **Tables**, **Queries**, or **Both** to display their contents.

3. Select a specific table or query, and click **Next**. A dialog box with the available fields will be displayed.

4. Select the field you would like to include in the lookup column, and click the **right arrow** to add the field to the Selected Fields box, as shown in Figure 3-9. Continue this process until you have chosen all the desired fields. If you would like to remove any of the fields from the selected field box simply select the field and click the **left arrow**. Click **Next**.

5. Choose to sort field(s) by ascending or descending order, steps shown in Figure 3-10. Click **Next**.

6. Adjust the column width for your lookup fields with the next step of the wizard. Do this by placing the cursor near the right edge of the column. When a double-headed arrow appears, drag the column to the desired width. Click **Next** when satisfied with the results. The last dialog box will be displayed.

7. Select the default label for the Lookup column or type in a new name. Click **Finish**.

8. Click **Save** and select **Datasheet view** to enter data using the Lookup Column.

TIP

To use a lookup column, open the drop-down list by selecting the arrow at the right of the text box. Scroll the list and click on the value you want to use.

Figure 3-9: You can choose multiple fields in the second step of the Lookup Wizard.

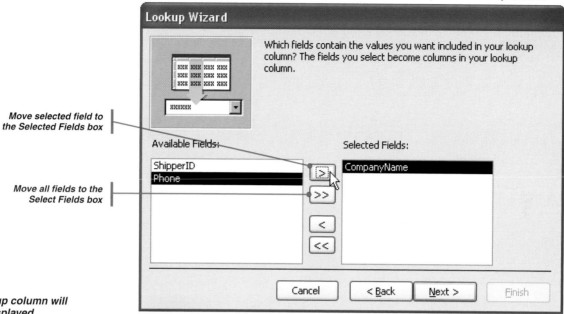

Move selected field to the Selected Fields box

Move all fields to the Select Fields box

Figure 3-10: The sort order of the lookup column will impact the order in which fields are displayed.

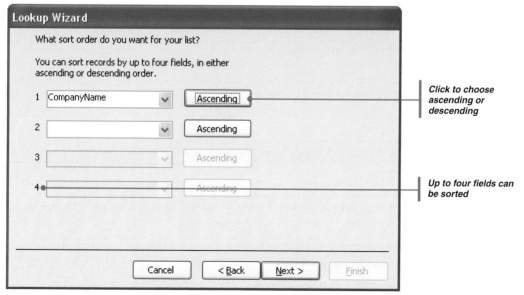

Click to choose ascending or descending

Up to four fields can be sorted

CREATE YOUR OWN VALUE LIST WITH THE LOOKUP WIZARD

This option allows you to have a set group of values from which you can choose when entering data.

1. Display the Lookup Wizard dialog box (see Steps 1-3 of "Use the Lookup Wizard").

2. Select **I Will Type In The Values That I Want**, and click **Next**.

3. Type your first value in the empty field, and press **TAB**. Continue entering values until your list is complete. If multiple columns of data are desired, enter the appropriate number in the **Number Of Columns** text box.

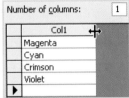

4. Adjust the column width by placing the cursor near the right edge of the column. When a double-headed arrow appears, drag the column to the desired width. Click **Next** when satisfied with the results. The last dialog box will be displayed.

5. Select the default label for the lookup column, or type in a new name. Click **Finish**.

6. Click **Save** and select **Datasheet View** to enter data using the lookup column.

EDIT THE LOOKUP LIST

After entering your data in a lookup list, you may find you need to add an additional item to this list.

1. Open a table in Design view.

2. Click the field with the lookup column.

3. Click the **Lookup** tab in the Field Properties area.

4. In the Row Source text box:

- **Add additional values** to the end of your list by typing the values enclosed in double quotation marks ("value") and separated with semicolons ("value1";"value2").

- **Delete any values** in your list by selecting the entire value, including quotation marks and semicolon, and press **DELETE**.

5. Click **Save** and select **Datasheet View** to enter data using the lookup column.

TIP

To expand all subdatasheets in the current table open, click **Format | Subdatasheets | Expand All**. To collapse all subdatasheets, follow a similar path: **Forms | Subdatasheets | Collapse All**.

Display and Create Subdatasheets

Access has the ability to display datasheets embedded within other datasheets. This can be established when a one-to-many relationship is defined between tables. See "Relate Tables," in Chapter 2 for more information on relating tables. The subdatasheet is actually the "many" side table of the one-to-many relationship.

View a Subdatasheet

In Datasheet view, open a table that contains a subdatasheet. You will recognize the existence of a subdatasheet by seeing plus signs in the far right column of your table, as displayed in Figure 3-11.

Figure 3-11: The subdatasheet provides details regarding the selected item.

Expands the subdatasheet

Contracts the subdatasheet

Subdatasheet provides detail

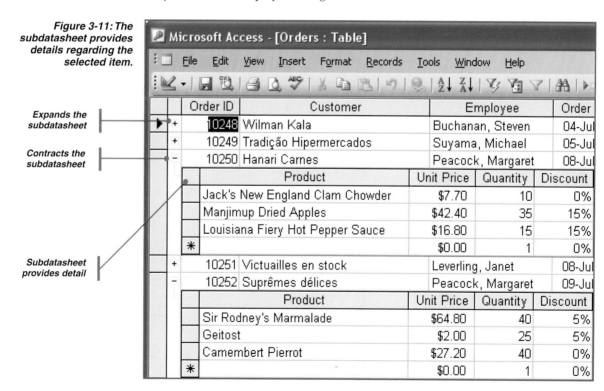

- Click the **plus sign** (+) next to the record you would like to explore. A subdatasheet providing details on that record is displayed.
- Click the **minus sign** (–) to hide the subdatatsheet.

TIP

To remove a subdatasheet click **Format | Subdatasheets | Remove**. This will not delete any information in the table.

Create a Subdatasheet

The subdatasheet can be useful in basic databases. Performance is sometimes negatively impacted in larger production type applications when the subdatasheet is included. This is due to the amount of information Access must pull in before displaying the datasheet. For smaller database scenarios, the subdatasheet can provide easy access to many data sources.

It is sometimes helpful to open the Relationships window in order to view the one-to-many relationships within a database, as shown in Figure 3-12.

Figure 3-12: The Relationships window displays the one-to-many relationships between tables.

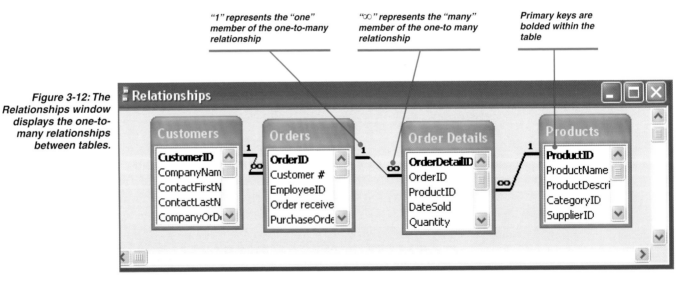

"1" represents the "one" member of the one-to-many relationship

"∞" represents the "many" member of the one-to many relationship

Primary keys are bolded within the table

1. Close all tables and open the Database window. Click the **Relationships** button to display the database relationships, as shown in Figure 3-12.

2. Note the one and many members of the tables. Close the **Relationships** window.

3. Open a table that is on the one side of a one-to-many relationship. In Datasheet view, click **Insert | Subdatasheet**. The Insert Subdatasheet dialog box will be displayed.

If you want to print the Relationships window, you can do so by using the Print Relationships Wizard. From within the Relationships window click **File | Print Relationships**. This will automatically create a report preview of the Relationships window. Select **File | Print** to print your Relationships window report.

NOTE

4. Click the table that will provide data for the subdatasheet. Try to select one of the tables on the "many" end of the relationship, as shown in Figure 3-12.

5. Click the **Link Child Fields down arrow**, and select a foreign key field (see Chapter 2 for information on foreign keys) in the subdatasheet table.

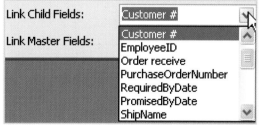

3

6. Click the **Link Master Fields down arrow**, and select the primary key field. The key fields should be the default view choice. Click **OK**.

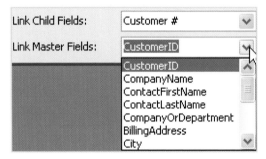

7. The Datasheet view will be displayed with plus signs at the far right side, indicating that subdatasheets are linked. Click the **plus signs** to view the subdatasheets, as shown in Figure 3-11.

Chapter 4

Working in the Datasheet

In this chapter you will learn how to add data to a table in Datasheet view, as shown in Figure 4-1, which includes acquiring data from external sources.

You will also see how to modify data you add to the datasheet by using editing techniques that include moving and copying, locating and replacing data, using a dictionary to flag spelling mistakes, and automatically correcting data as you type.

Additionally, you will learn how to format the datasheet to better present the data or emphasize just the data you want to see.

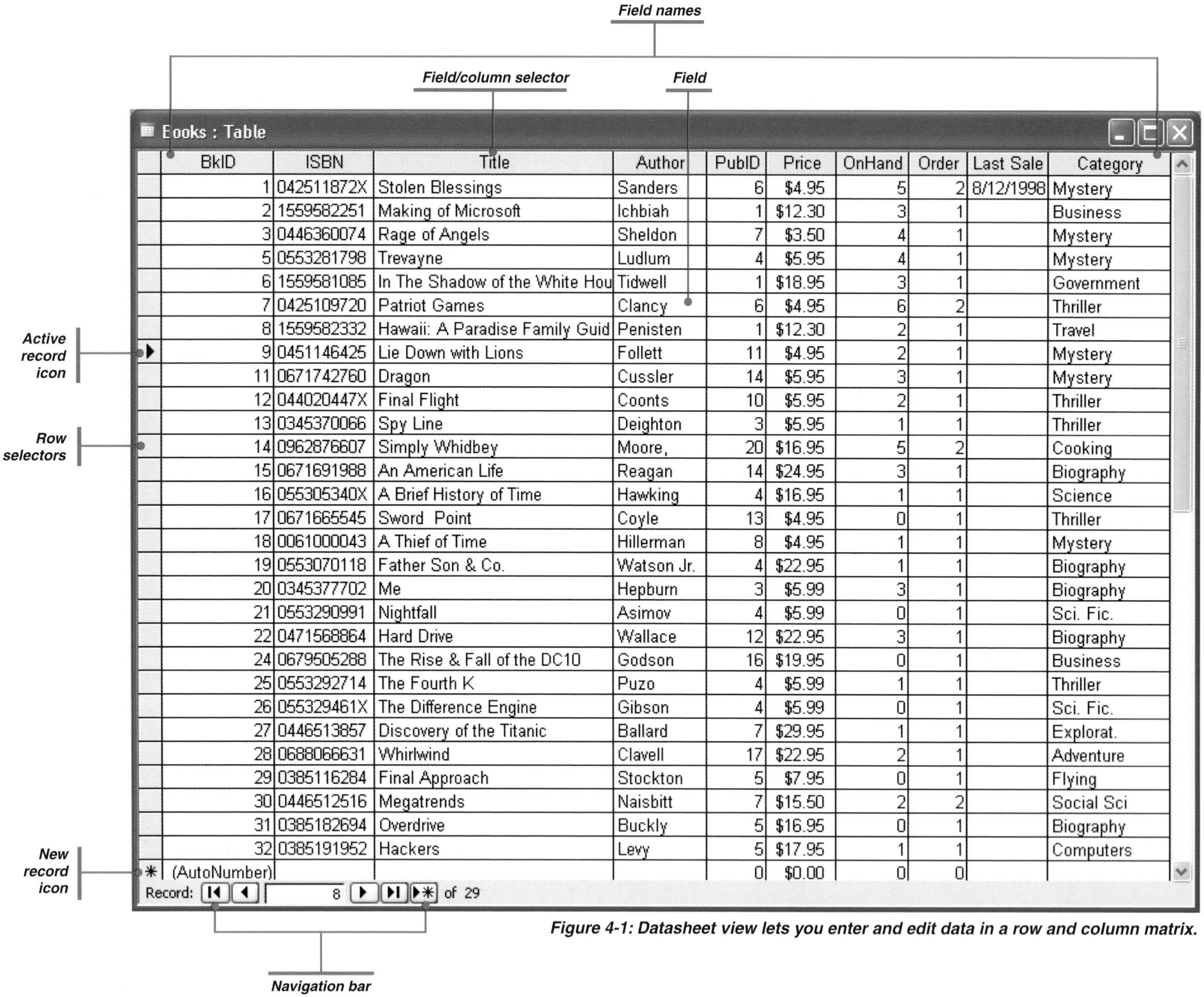

Field names

Field/column selector   Field

Books : Table

	BkID	ISBN	Title	Author	PubID	Price	OnHand	Order	Last Sale	Category
	1	042511872X	Stolen Blessings	Sanders	6	$4.95	5	2	8/12/1998	Mystery
	2	1559582251	Making of Microsoft	Ichbiah	1	$12.30	3	1		Business
	3	0446360074	Rage of Angels	Sheldon	7	$3.50	4	1		Mystery
	5	0553281798	Trevayne	Ludlum	4	$5.95	4	1		Mystery
	6	1559581085	In The Shadow of the White Hou	Tidwell	1	$18.95	3	1		Government
	7	0425109720	Patriot Games	Clancy	6	$4.95	6	2		Thriller
	8	1559582332	Hawaii: A Paradise Family Guid	Penisten	1	$12.30	2	1		Travel
▶	9	0451146425	Lie Down with Lions	Follett	11	$4.95	2	1		Mystery
	11	0671742760	Dragon	Cussler	14	$5.95	3	1		Mystery
	12	044020447X	Final Flight	Coonts	10	$5.95	2	1		Thriller
	13	0345370066	Spy Line	Deighton	3	$5.95	1	1		Thriller
	14	0962876607	Simply Whidbey	Moore,	20	$16.95	5	2		Cooking
	15	0671691988	An American Life	Reagan	14	$24.95	3	1		Biography
	16	055305340X	A Brief History of Time	Hawking	4	$16.95	1	1		Science
	17	0671665545	Sword Point	Coyle	13	$4.95	0	1		Thriller
	18	0061000043	A Thief of Time	Hillerman	8	$4.95	1	1		Mystery
	19	0553070118	Father Son & Co.	Watson Jr.	4	$22.95	1	1		Biography
	20	0345377702	Me	Hepburn	3	$5.99	3	1		Biography
	21	0553290991	Nightfall	Asimov	4	$5.99	0	1		Sci. Fic.
	22	0471568864	Hard Drive	Wallace	12	$22.95	3	1		Biography
	24	0679505288	The Rise & Fall of the DC10	Godson	16	$19.95	0	1		Business
	25	0553292714	The Fourth K	Puzo	4	$5.99	1	1		Thriller
	26	055329461X	The Difference Engine	Gibson	4	$5.99	0	1		Sci. Fic.
	27	0446513857	Discovery of the Titanic	Ballard	7	$29.95	1	1		Explorat.
	28	0688066631	Whirlwind	Clavell	17	$22.95	2	1		Adventure
	29	0385116284	Final Approach	Stockton	5	$7.95	0	1		Flying
	30	0446512516	Megatrends	Naisbitt	7	$15.50	2	2		Social Sci
	31	0385182694	Overdrive	Buckly	5	$16.95	0	1		Biography
	32	0385191952	Hackers	Levy	5	$17.95	1	1		Computers
*	(AutoNumber)					$0.00	0	0		

Record: ◀◀ ◀ 8 ▶ ▶▶ ▶* of 29

Active record icon

Row selectors

New record icon

Navigation bar

Figure 4-1: Datasheet view lets you enter and edit data in a row and column matrix.

Enter and Edit Data

Data is Access's *raison d'etre* (or reason to be), yet before we can organize the data, retrieve it, present it, or otherwise *use* it, we have to get it into a table. Chapters 2 and 3 described how to create a database, set up a table design, and change the properties of the table fields so data entered into the table will conform to formatting, input masks, and other rules you establish. This section will show you ways to populate a designed table with new data.

Enter New Data in a Datasheet

You use the keyboard to type new data into the datasheet. If you are adding data to a newly created table, you will be positioned at the first field in the first record, and you can just start adding data. If you are adding data to a datasheet with existing data, you will need to create a new record at the end of the datasheet and start adding data there.

1. Open the database and select **Tables** in the Database window.

2. Create a table using one of the wizards (see Chapters 2 and 3 on how to create and design a table), or double-click an existing database to open it.

Use to open a blank datasheet

Double-click an existing table to open it in Datasheet view

ENTER NEW DATA TO A BLANK DATASHEET

You will see the field names in the row across the top of the datasheet, an empty matrix, the active record pointer in the first data row, and the insertion point in the first field of the first record.

1. Type the value you want in the first field and press **TAB**. If you do not have a value to add to a field (you do not have to type a value in a field unless the field has a field property requiring you to do so), press **TAB** until the insertion point is in the field you want, or click the next field you want to enter a value into.

2. Repeat until you reach the last field you want to add a value to in the current record. Press **TAB** or click the first field where you want to add data in the next blank record.

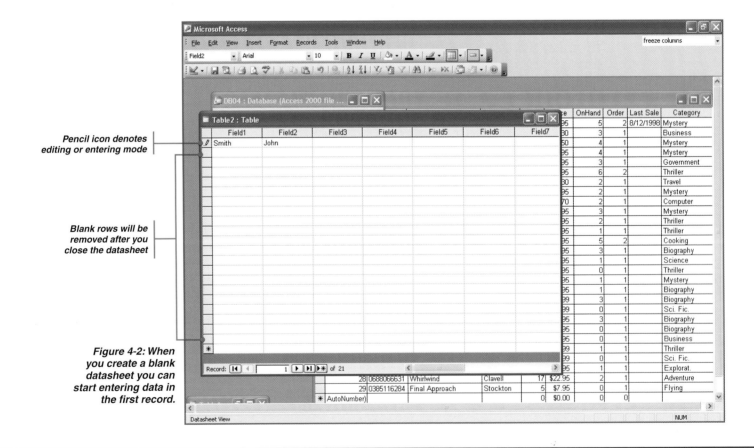

Pencil icon denotes editing or entering mode

Blank rows will be removed after you close the datasheet

Figure 4-2: When you create a blank datasheet you can start entering data in the first record.

You can also press ENTER to move from one field to the next. If you find you are not experiencing this behavior, open **Tools | Options | Keyboard**, and under Move After Edit, select **Next Field**, or choose the option you want. Click **OK** when finished.

Move after enter
- ○ Don't move
- ● Next field
- ○ Next record

Many shortcut key combinations work differently depending on whether Access considers you are navigating through or editing data. For example, when an entire field's value is selected (or the insertion point is at the end of the value), pressing RIGHT ARROW moves the selection to the next field to the right. If you click a field's value, placing the insertion point in the value, pressing RIGHT ARROW moves the insertion point one character to the right. Press F2 to toggle from one mode to the other. Table 4-1 lists the navigation mode options.

ENTER NEW DATA TO AN EXISTING DATASHEET

The last blank row in the datasheet, identified with a large asterisk in its row selector, is the new record row into which you add new data.

| | | 29 | 0385116284 | Final Approach |
| * | AutoNumber) | | | |

Record: |◀ ◀ 5 ▶ ▶| ▶* of 28

1. Do one of the following:
   - Click a field in the new record row.
   - Click the new record button on the navigation bar. ▶*
   - Click **New Record** on the Table Datasheet toolbar. ▶
   - Open the **Edit** menu, point to **Go To**, and click **New Record**.
   - Press **CTRL++ (CTRL** and the plus sign**)**.

2. Type the value you want in the first field, and press **TAB**. If you do not have a value to add to a field (you do not have to type a value in a field unless the field has a field property requiring you to do so), press **TAB** until the insertion point is in the field you want, or click the next field you want to enter a value into.

   As soon as you start typing in the new record row, a new row is added to the bottom of the datasheet.

Use Keyboard Shortcuts in a Datasheet

Data entry is largely done using the keyboard. Becoming familiar with using the keyboard for other related tasks can be quite a time-saver.

USE THE KEYBOARD TO NAVIGATE

Table 4-1 lists several of the more commonly used keyboard shortcuts for navigating in a datasheet.

MOVING THROUGH RECORDS

The navigation bar at the bottom of a datasheet window and the Go To option on the Edit menu provide several options for quickly getting to the record you want in a datasheet.

MOVE TO THE FIRST RECORD

- Click the first record button on the navigation bar. ⏮
  –Or–
- Click the **Edit** menu, select **Go To**, and click **First**.

MOVE TO THE LAST RECORD

- Click the last record button on the navigation bar. ⏭
  –Or–
- Click the **Edit** menu, select **Go To**, and click **Last**.

MOVE TO THE NEXT RECORD

- Click the next record button on the navigation bar. ▶
  –Or–
- Click the **Edit** menu, select **Go To**, and click **Next**.

MOVE TO THE PREVIOUS RECORD

- Click the previous record button on the navigation bar. ◀
  –Or–
- Click the **Edit** menu, select **Go To**, and click **Previous**.

MOVE TO A SPECIFIC RECORD

Type the record number in the navigation bar text box, and press **ENTER**.

TABLE 4-1: SHORTCUTS FOR NAVIGATING IN A DATASHEET

TO MOVE...	PRESS...
To the next (to the right) field	**TAB**, **RIGHT ARROW**, or **ENTER** (see the Tip on changing the behavior of using **ENTER** in the datasheet)
To the previous (to the left) field	**SHIFT+TAB** or **LEFT ARROW**
To the last field in the active record	**END**
To the first field in the active record	**HOME**
Up one record at a time in the same field	**UP ARROW**
Up to the first record in the same field	**CTRL+UP ARROW**
Up one screen	**PAGE UP**
Down one record at a time in the same field	**DOWN ARROW**
Down to the last record in the same field	**CTRL+DOWN ARROW**
Down one screen	**PAGE DOWN**
The first field in the first record	**CTRL+HOME**
The last field in the last record	**CTRL+END**
Right one screen	**CTRL+PAGE DOWN**
Left one screen	**CTRL+PAGE UP**

TIP

If you don't see an insertion point in the datasheet, press **F2**.

USE THE KEYBOARD TO INSERT DATA

Table 4-2 lists several shortcuts for inserting commonly used information and performing other tasks.

TABLE 4-2: SHORTCUTS FOR INSERTING COMMONLY USED INFORMATION

TO...	PRESS...
Add a new record	CTRL++
Delete the current record	CTRL+-
Insert the current time	CTRL+SHIFT+:
Insert the current date	CTRL+;
Insert the same value from the record's previous field	CTRL+'

USE THE KEYBOARD TO EDIT DATA

Table 4-3 lists shortcuts for editing data.

TABLE 4-3: SHORTCUTS FOR EDITING DATA

TO...	PRESS...
Undo a typing action	CTRL+Z
Cancel typing actions in a record	ESC (pressing once cancels actions in the current field; pressing a second time cancels actions for the record)
Delete the character to the left of the insertion point	BACKSPACE
Delete the character to the right of the insertion point	DELETE
Delete all characters in a word to the right of the insertion point	CTRL+DELETE
Move one character to the right (if this takes you one field to the right, press **F2**)	RIGHT ARROW
Move one character to the left (if this takes you one field to the left, press **F2**)	LEFT ARROW
Move to the beginning of the next word to the right	CTRL+RIGHT ARROW
Move to the beginning of the previous word to the left	CTRL+LEFT ARROW
Move to the end of the field	END
Move to the beginning of the field	HOME

TIP

Windows computers come with a built-in *Extend* mode that make selecting fields and records even easier than the standard shortcuts. Press **F8** to enable Extend mode. You will see EXT displayed toward the right end of the status bar. Now when a field or record is selected, you can extend that selection by using the arrow keys. (If the behavior doesn't work, press **F2**.) Press **ESC** to stop using Extend mode.

QUICKSTEPS

SELECTING RECORDS, FIELDS, AND COLUMNS WITH THE MOUSE

Open a table in Datasheet view.

SELECT RECORDS

- To select a single record, click the record selector to the left of the record, or place the insertion point in the record and click **Edit | Select Record**. The record becomes highlighted.

- To select adjacent records, point at the first/last row in the group you want to select. When the mouse pointer becomes a rightward pointing arrow, drag over the record selectors of the records. The selected rows are reverse highlighted (white text on black background).

Books : Table		
BkID	ISBN	Title
1	042511872X	Stolen Blessings
2	1559582251	Making of Microsoft
3	0446360074	Rage of Angels
5	0553281798	Trevayne
6	1559581085	In The Shadow of the W
7	0425109720	Patriot Games
8	1559582332	Hawaii: A Paradise Far
9	0451146425	Lie Down with Lions

To select all records, click **Edit | Select All Records**.

Continued...

USE THE KEYBOARD TO SELECT DATA

Table 4-4 list shortcuts for selecting data.

TABLE 4-4: SHORTCUTS FOR SELECTING DATA

TO...	PRESS...
Select a character to the right	SHIFT+RIGHT ARROW
Select a character to the left	SHIFT+LEFT ARROW
Select remaining characters in a word to the right	CTRL+SHIFT+RIGHT ARROW
Select remaining characters in a word to the left	CTRL+SHIFT+LEFT ARROW
Select the next field	TAB
Select record above a selected record	SHIFT+UP ARROW
Select record below a selected record	SHIFT+DOWN ARROW
Select all records	CTRL+A

Insert Pictures

You can insert pictures, such as .jpg and .bmp files, in your datasheet, though you will have to create a form to see the image. See Chapter 6 to learn how to create forms.

1. Open the table in Datasheet view.

2. Right-click a field in a column that is formatted with an OLE Object data type, and select **Insert Object**. See Chapter 3 for information on the OLE Object data type and how to change a column's data type.

3. In the object dialog box, shown in Figure 4-3, select **Create From File**. Click **Browse** to open the Browse dialog box, locate, and select the graphic you want to add. Click **OK**.

4. In the object dialog box, do either:

   - Select the **Link** check box to create an OLE (object linking and embedding) link between the source picture file and the file in the datasheet. Whenever the source file is changed, the changes will be reflected in the picture in the datasheet.

   - Deselect the **Link** check box to embed a copy of the picture in the datasheet. Changes to the source file will not affect the picture in the datasheet.

SELECTING RECORDS, FIELDS, AND COLUMNS WITH THE MOUSE

(Continued)

SELECT DATA IN A FIELD

- To select partial data in a field, drag over the characters you want.

SELECT FIELDS

- To select a single field, point at the left edge of the field, and when the cursor changes to a large cross, click your mouse button.

1X	The Differer
57	Discovery c
31	Whirlwind

- To select adjacent fields, point at the left edge of the first field, and when the cursor changes to a large cross, drag left or right across the fields you want to select.

SELECT COLUMNS

- To select all fields in a column, click the field selector (the box that contains the field name) at the top of the column.

- To select adjacent columns, point at the column selector in the first column to be selected, and when the cursor changes to a down arrow, drag left or right across the columns you want selected.

Title	Author ⇩	PubID
Stolen Blessings	Sanders	6
Making of Microsoft	Ichbiah	1

5. Click **OK**. A placeholder with a connection to the image is placed in the field. To view the image, right-click the field, point at **Package Object**, and select **Activate Contents**. The image will open in a graphics program.

Figure 4-3: After locating a picture and other graphic in this dialog box, a placeholder is added to the field in the datasheet.

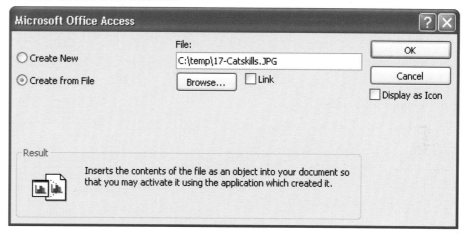

Copy and Move Data

You can duplicate or remove data within a datasheet by using the standard copy, cut, and paste techniques; however, there are a few twists that Access imposes. (See "Use Keyboard Shortcuts in a Datasheet" and the QuickSteps, "Selecting Records, Fields, and Columns with the Mouse," for ways to select fields and records.)

COPY AND MOVE CHARACTERS

1. In Datasheet view, select the characters you want to copy or move.

2. Do either:

- Click **Edit | Copy** or click **Copy** on the Table Datasheet toolbar to make a duplicate of the selected data and leave the original data in place.

- Click **Edit | Cut** or click **Cut** on the Table Datasheet toolbar to make a duplicate of the selected data and remove the original data.

3. In the destination field, either place your insertion point where you want the new characters inserted or select characters that will be overwritten by the new characters.

4. Click **Edit | Paste** or click **Paste** on the Table Datasheet toolbar to complete the action.

COPY AND MOVE FIELDS

In Datasheet view, select the fields you want to copy or move.

1. Do either:

   • Click **Edit | Copy** or click **Copy** on the Table Datasheet toolbar to make a duplicate of the selected data and leave the original data in place.

   • Click **Edit | Cut** or click **Cut** on the Table Datasheet toolbar to make a duplicate of the selected data and remove the original data.

2. Select an equivalent block of fields where you want the new data. For example, if you selected three adjacent fields in a record that you wanted to copy, ensure that you select three adjacent destination fields where you want the data pasted.

3. Click **Edit | Paste** or click **Paste** on the Table Datasheet toolbar to complete the action. Any existing data in the destination fields will be overwritten by the new data.

COPY OR MOVE RECORDS

In Datasheet view, select the records you want to copy or move.

1. Do either:

   • Click **Edit | Copy** or click **Copy** on the Table Datasheet toolbar to make a duplicate of the selected records and leave the original records in place.

   • Click **Edit | Cut** or click **Cut** on the Table Datasheet toolbar to make a duplicate of the selected records and remove the original records.

2. Click **Edit | Paste Append**. The copied or moved records will be added to the end of the datasheet.

USE THE OFFICE CLIPBOARD

The Office Clipboard retains up to 24 of your latest copy items that you can paste into the datasheet.

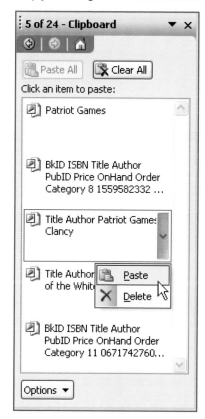

Figure 4-4: The Office Clipboard task pane "remembers" your last 24 copy actions, so you can repeat one by simply selecting Paste from its menu.

1. In Datasheet view, select the fields you want to copy, and either click **Edit | Copy** or click **Copy** on the Table Datasheet toolbar.

2. Select an equivalent block of fields where you want the new data pasted.

3. Click **Edit | Office Clipboard** to display the Clipboard task pane.

4. Point at the item you want copied, click the **down arrow**, and then select **Paste** from the menu, as shown in Figure 4-4.

Delete Records and Columns

In Access, unlike most programs, when you remove data by deleting records and columns, you cannot undo your actions. However, Access will ask you to confirm your deletions before they are irretrievably gone.

DELETE RECORDS

1. Select the record(s) you want to delete (see "Use the Keyboard to Edit Data" and the QuickSteps, "Selecting Fields and Records with the Mouse," for way to select records and fields).

2. Click **Delete Record** on the Table Datasheet toolbar; or right-click the selection and click **Delete Record**.

3. Click **Yes** to confirm your deletion.

DELETE COLUMNS

1. Select the column(s) you want to delete (see "Use the Keyboard to Edit Data" and the QuickSteps, "Selecting Fields and Records with the Mouse," for ways to select records and fields).

TIP

If you click **Delete Record** without selecting a record, the active record will be deleted.

2. Right-click the selection and click **Delete Column**, or click **Edit | Delete Column**.

3. Click **Yes** to confirm your deletion.

Find and Replace Text

In datasheets that might span thousands of rows and columns, you need the ability to locate data quickly as well as find instances of the same data so consistent replacements can be made.

FIND DATA

1. Open a table in Datasheet view.

2. Click **Find** on the Table Datasheet toolbar, or press **CTRL+F** to open the Find And  Replace dialog box Find tab, shown in Figure 4-5.

3. Type the characters you want to find in the Find What text box.

4. Click the **Look In down arrow** and choose whether to search the entire table or just the field where the insertion point is currently located.

Look In:	Books : Table ∨
Match:	Author
	Books : Table

5. Click the **Match down arrow** and choose one of the following:

   - **Any Part Of Field** to locate fields that contain the searched for characters embedded in any text within a field (For example, searching for "pen" would find fields that contained "opening.")

   - **Whole Field** to locate fields that contain only the searched for characters (For example, searching for "pen" would find fields that contained only "pen.")

   - **Start Of Field** to locate fields that contain the searched for characters at the beginning of the field (For example, searching for "pen" would find fields that contained "Penn Station.")

6. Click the **Search down arrow** to determine the scope of the search. Choose:

   - **All** to search the entire datasheet

   - **Up** to search from the current insertion point location toward the first record

   - **Down** to search from the current insertion point location toward the last record

7. Select the **Match Case** check box to only find fields that match the case of the characters (For example, searching for "pen" would not find "Penn Station.")

8. Click **Find Next**.

Figure 4-5: The Find tab lets you refine your search based on several criteria.

REPLACE DATA

The Replace tab of the Find And Replace dialog box looks and behaves similar to the Find tab covered earlier.

1. Open a table in Datasheet view.

2. Click **Find** on the Table Datasheet toolbar, or press **CTRL+F** to open the Find And Replace dialog box. Click the **Replace** tab.

3. Type the characters you want to be found and replaced in the Find What text box.

4. Type the replacement characters in the Replace With text box. If specific search criteria are needed, see "Find Data" for the options descriptions. Do either:

   ● Click **Find Next** and then click **Replace** to make replacement one a time.

   ● Click **Replace All** to perform all replacements at once.

Verify Spelling

You can check spelling of selected fields, columns, records, or the entire datasheet using Access' main dictionary and a custom dictionary you add words to. (Both are shared with other Office programs).

1. Open a table in Datasheet view.

2. Select the fields, columns, or records to check. If nothing is selected, the entire datasheet will be checked.

3. Click **Tools | Spelling**. When the spell checker doesn't find anything to report, you are told the spelling check is complete. Otherwise, the Spelling dialog box opens as shown in Figure 4-6.

4. With a highlighted word in the Not In Dictionary/Capitalization text box, you may change the characters by picking from the Suggestions list and clicking **Change** or **Change All** to replace the current or all occurrences of the highlighted word. If you have a correct term that is not found in the dictionary, you may:

   - Click **Ignore Field Name** to discontinue searching in the current column for mis-spelled or incorrectly capitalized words.

   - Click **Ignore** to disregard the current occurrence of the word shown in the Not In Dictionary/Capitalization text box.

   - Click **Ignore All** to disregard all occurrences of the word shown in the Not In Dictionary/Capitalization text box.

5. Click **AutoCorrect** if you want to automatically replace words in the future. (See "Modify Automatic Corrections," later in this chapter, for more information on using AutoCorrect.)

6. Click **Options** to change language or custom dictionaries and to set other spelling criteria.

TIP

If the correct spelling of a misspelled word is not shown in the Suggestions list box, edit the word in the Not In Dictionary text box, and click **Add** to include it in a custom dictionary that is checked in addition to the main dictionary.

Figure 4-6: The Spelling dialog box provides several options to handle misspelled or uncommon words.

MODIFY AUTOMATIC CORRECTIONS

Access automatically corrects common data entry mistakes as you type, replacing characters and words you choose with other choices. You can control how this is done.

1. Open a table in Datasheet view.

2. Click **Tools | Options**, choose the Spelling tab, and click **AutoCorrect Options**. The AutoCorrect dialog box opens, as shown in Figure 4-7. As appropriate, do one or more:

   • Choose the type of automatic corrections you do or do not want from the options at the top of the dialog box.

   • Click **Exceptions** to set capitalization exceptions.

   • Click **Replace Text As You Type** to turn off automatic text replacement (turned on by default).

   • Add new words or characters to the Replace and With lists and click **Add**, or select a current item in the list, edit it, and click **Replace**.

   • Delete replacement text by selecting the item in the Replace With list and clicking **Delete**.

3. Click **OK** when you are done.

NOTE

You can also add data into a table from another table, in
either the current database or another Access database,
by using an Append Query. See Chapter 5 for more
information on using queries.

Acquire Data

In addition to typing data directly into a datasheet, you can enter data by using
a form (see Chapter 6) or get existing data into a datasheet by:

- Importing from several different sources into a new or existing Access table
- Copying and pasting

Once the data is "safely" in your Access datasheet/table, you have all the tools
and features this book describes to format, organize, analyze, retrieve, and
otherwise convert the *data* into the *information* you want.

Import Data from Outside Sources

Most data types use a similar Import Wizard to guide you through the importing process, shown in Figure 4-8. The data types you can import from are:

- dBASE III, IV, 5
- Microsoft Outlook
- Delimited/fixed width text files
- ODBC-compliant databases
- Exchange
- Paradox
- Lotus 1-2-3

- SharePoint Team Services
- Microsoft Access
- Web pages
- Microsoft Excel
- Windows SharePoint Services
- Microsoft Exchange
- XML pages

TIP

Importing data into Access tables is a one-shot process—that is, you get whatever data is in the source at the moment you import. You can maintain a real time connection to external data if you *link* it to an Access table. Linking data, and other data exchange, is covered in Chapter 10.

Figure 4-8: A similar Import Wizard guides you through the process of adding data from several sources.

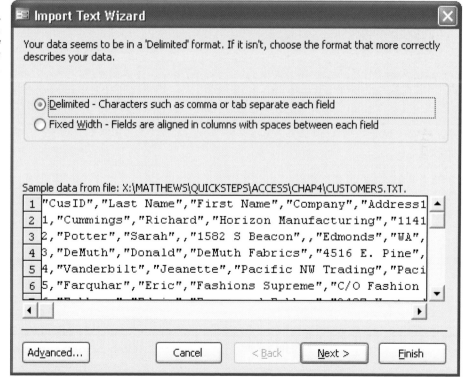

CAUTION

You can click **Finish** at any time in the various Import wizards. Doing so certainly expedites the process, but it may overwrite existing data in your currently selected table, causing irreversible changes.

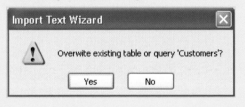

IMPORT DATA FROM TEXT FILES

Text files are files with file extensions such as .txt and .csv (comma-separated values) that can be formatted using commas, spaces, tabs, and other separators to organize their data. Though the data may not appear to be structured, as shown in Figure 4-8, Access can correctly place the data in columns as long as the data is separated in a consistent and recognizable format.

1. Open the database into which you want to add the data from the text file. If you know you want to add the data to an existing table, select that table in the Database window.

2. Click **File | Get External Data | Import** to display the Import dialog box. Click the **Files Of Type down arrow** and select **Text Files…** to limit which files you will see. Browse to the folder that contains the text file you want, select the text file, and click **Import**.

Files of type: Text Files (*.txt;*.csv;*.tab;*.asc)

3. In the first dialog box of the Import Text Wizard, preview the file in the lower half of the dialog box. If all appears to be in order, Access has done a good job so far. If not, try choosing the other format. In any case, click **Next** to continue with other options.

4. The second Import Text Wizard dialog box lets you fine tune the delimiter used or set fixed-length widths, depending on your choice in the previous dialog box. Select **First Row Contains Field Names** if your text file is set up that way. Click **Next**.

5. In the third Import Text Wizard dialog box, choose where you want the data. Either:

   ● Click **In A New Table** and click **Next** to continue with Step 6.

   –Or–

   ● Click **If In An Existing Table**, click the **down arrow**, and select the table from the drop-down list. Click **Next** and then

   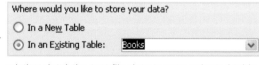

   click **Finish** to *append* (add to existing data) the text file data to your selected table.

6. In the fourth Import Text Wizard dialog box, you can set up field information about each column. To change field information for other than the first field, click the **Advanced** button and type the information in the Field Information area. Click **OK**, and your changes will be reflected in the wizard. If you do not want to bother with that now, you can modify the field information in Design view after the data has been imported. Click **Next** when finished.

7. In the fifth Import Text Wizard dialog box, choose whether, and how, to assign a primary key to the new table (see Chapter 2 for information on primary keys). Click **Next**.

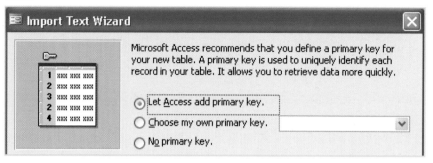

8. In the last Import Text Wizard dialog box, type a new name for the new table in the **Import To Table** text box, and click **Finish**.

IMPORT DATA FROM SPREADSHEETS

Data created by spreadsheet programs such as Microsoft Excel and Lotus 1-2-3 is imported using the Import Spreadsheet Wizard

1. Open the database into which you want to add the data from the text file. If you know you want to add the data to an existing table, select that table in the Database window.

2. Click **File | Get External Data | Import** to display the Import dialog box. Click the **Files Of Type down arrow** and select a spreadsheet program, such as Microsoft Excel, to limit which files you will see. Browse to the folder that contains the spreadsheet file you want, select the file, and click **Import**.

3. In the first dialog box of the Import Spreadsheet Wizard, shown in Figure 4-9, choose whether to get data from worksheets or named ranges. Select the item that contains the data, and preview the item in the lower half of the dialog box. Click **Next** to continue with other options.

4. The second Import Spreadsheet Wizard dialog box lets you use column headings for field names in Access. Select **First Row Contains Column Headings** if your data is set up that way. Click **Next**.

TIP

Access does a pretty good job choosing the correct data type for imported Excel data; however, you may want to change some data types on your own. Dates in Excel are generally formatted as numbers so they can be used in calculation—in Access dates are typically used in a Text data type.

5. In the third Import Spreadsheet Wizard dialog box, choose where you want the data. Either:

- Click **In A New Table** and click **Next** to continue with Step 6.

  –Or–

- Click **If In An Existing Table**, click the **down arrow**, and select the table from the drop-down list. Click **Next** and then click **Finish** to *append* (add to existing data) the data to your selected table.

6. In the fourth Import Spreadsheet Wizard dialog box, you can set up field information about each column. If you do not what to bother with that now, you can modify the field information in Design view after the data has been imported. Click **Next** when finished.

7. In the fifth Import Spreadsheet Wizard dialog box, choose whether, and how, to assign a primary key to the new table (see Chapter 2 for information on primary keys). Click **Next**.

8. In the last Import Spreadsheet Wizard dialog box, type a new name for the new table in the Import To Table text box, and click **Finish**.

Figure 4-9: Data from programs such as Microsoft Excel can be parsed into Access datasheets by sheets or named ranges.

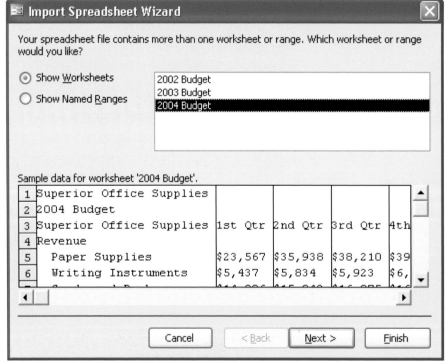

IMPORT ACCESS TABLES

You can import tables (and other Access objects) from other Access databases.

1. Open the database into which you want to add the data from the text file. If you know you want to add the data to an existing table, select that table in the Database window.

2. Click **File | Get External Data | Import** to display the Import dialog box. Click the **Files Of Type down arrow**, and select **Microsoft Office Access** to limit which files you will see. Browse to the folder that contains the database file you want, select the file, and click **Import**.

3. In the Import Objects dialog box, shown in Figure 4-10, select the table(s) whose data you want. If you need to deselect a choice, either click the table you want deselected or use the **Deselect All** button and start over.

4. Click the **Options** button. Under:

   - **Import**, select one or more of the features to include with the imported table(s)

   - **Import Tables**, choose whether to import the table's definition (design) and data, or just its definition

5. Click **OK**.

> ### TIP
>
> If you want to import just the field structure for an Access table—that is, a table without any data—select **Definition Only** in the Import Objects dialog box.

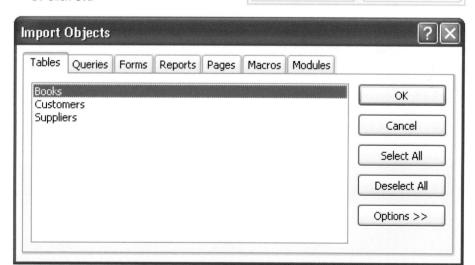

Figure 4-10: You can choose which table, as well as other objects, to import from an Access database.

NOTE

When pasting data into a table, it's very important to ensure that the field structure of the source and destination tables are the same so data isn't lost. For example, if your source record contains more fields than your destination table, the data in the additional fields is simply not added to the destination table. Also, the data types need to be compatible. If there is a data type mismatch, Access will display an error, similar to Figure 4-11. Also, data unable to be pasted will be added to a Paste Errors table.

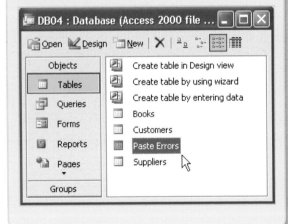

Paste Data into a Datasheet

You can add existing rows (records) or columns of data to your datasheet by pasting them from other data sources.

Figure 4-11: Pasted data needs to be of the same data type as that in your table.

1. Open the program that contains the data you want.

2. Select the rows or fields you want using the selection techniques of the source program.

3. Copy the data to the Windows Clipboard, either by clicking **Edit | Copy** or by clicking the **Copy** button on a toolbar.

4. Open the Access table into which you want to place the data in Datasheet view (See "Use Keyboard Shortcuts in a Datasheet" and the QuickSteps, "Selecting Records, Fields, and Columns with the Mouse," for ways to select fields and records.). Do one of the following:

   - To paste the data as new records to the end of the datasheet, click **Edit | Paste Append**.

   - To replace records, select the records to be replaced, and either click **Edit | Paste** or click **Paste** on the Table Datasheet toolbar.

   - To replace fields, select the fields to be replaced, and either click **Edit | Paste** or click **Paste** on the Table Datasheet toolbar.

Arrange the Datasheet

There are several actions you can take to customize how you see the data presented in a datasheet. You can resize rows and columns, hide columns, and format the appearance of the datasheet.

Insert Columns

You can insert blank columns or columns that are formatted with lookup or hyperlink data types. (See the QuickSteps, "Selecting Records, Fields, and Columns with the Mouse," for information on selecting columns.)

INSERT BLANK COLUMNS

1. Click the column selector for the column to the right of where you want to add a new blank column.

2. Right-click the selected column and select **Insert Column** from the context menu. A new column is added to the left of your selected column.

Field1	PubID
	6
	1
	7
	4

3. Rename the column name as necessary (see "Rename a Column," later in this chapter).

Figure 4-12: The Lookup Wizard helps you add items to a drop-down list by pulling them from tables or queries or by allowing you to type them in.

INSERT A LOOKUP COLUMN

1. Click the column selector for the column to the right of where you want to add a lookup column.

2. Right-click the selected column and select **Lookup Column** from the context menu. The Lookup Wizard opens, as shown in Figure 4-12.

3. Choose whether to pull lookup items from a table or query or to add your own items. Click **Next** and follow the instructions in the wizard (see Chapter 3 for specifics on using the Lookup Wizard).

4. Click **Finish** in the last wizard dialog box. The lookup column is added to the left of the selected column.

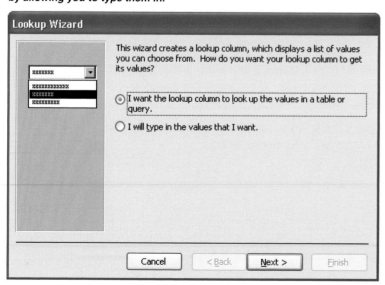

Lookup Wizard

This wizard creates a lookup column, which displays a list of values you can choose from. How do you want your lookup column to get its values?

⊙ I want the lookup column to look up the values in a table or query.

○ I will type in the values that I want.

[Cancel] [< Back] [Next >] [Finish]

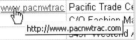
INSERT A HYPERLINK COLUMN

1. Click the column selector for the column to the right of where you want to add a hyperlink column.

2. Click **Insert | Hyperlink Column**. A seemingly blank column is added to the left of the select column.

3. Add data to the column. Any added data will be displayed as a hyperlink, though the target of the link will need to be provided.

Company	Field1
Horizon Manufa	www.horizonma
DeMuth Fabrics	www.demuthfab
Pacific NW Trac	www.pacnwtrac
Fashions Supre	

4. Right-click a value in the hyperlink column, point at **Hyperlink**, and select **Edit Hyperlink**. In the Edit Hyperlink dialog box, locate the destination for the link (see Chapters 3 and 10 for more information on setting up hyperlinks). Click **OK**.

5. Rename the column name as necessary (see "Rename a Column" later in this chapter).

Adjust Column Width

There are several ways to change the width of a column:

- By using the mouse to drag the column to the width you want
- By typing a precise width
- By letting Access choose a default or tailored width

CHANGE THE WIDTH FOR A SINGLE COLUMN WITH THE MOUSE

1. Point at the right border of the column selector until the pointer changes to a cross with left and right arrowheads

↔ Author
Sanders

2. Drag the border to the left or right to the width you want.

↔	Author
igs	Sanders

UICKSTEPS

CHANGING HOW THE CURRENT DATASHEET LOOKS

Unlike spreadsheets and Word tables, formatting is applied on an entire datasheet basis—that is, you cannot format individual fields, rows, or columns when working in Datasheet view. (You can do limited formatting of columns by using field properties in Design view, as described in Chapter 3). Click **View | Toolbars | Formatting (Datasheet)** to view formatting options for the current datasheet.

CHANGE TEXT ATTRIBUTES

- To change the typeface, click the **Font down arrow**, scroll the list, and select a new typeface.

  Arial ▾

- To change text size, click the **Font Size down arrow**, scroll the list, and select a new size.

  10 ▾

- To bold, italicize, or underline field contents, click the respective button.

  B *I* U

- To change text color, click the **Font/Fore Color down arrow**, and select a color from the palette. Recently used colors appear at the bottom of the palette.

  A ▾

Continued...

CHANGE THE WIDTH FOR ADJACENT COLUMNS WITH THE MOUSE

When you change the column width for a group of selected columns, the widths of each column are changed by the same amount.

1. Select the columns whose widths you want to adjust.
2. Drag the right border of any of the selected columns to the left or right to the width you want.

CHANGE THE WIDTH OF COLUMNS PRECISELY

1. Select the column(s) whose width you want to adjust.
2. Right-click the selection and select **Column Width**.
3. In the Column Width dialog box, type a column width (15.67 is the default width for the default font), and click **OK**.

LET ACCESS DETERMINE THE COLUMN WIDTH

1. Select the column(s) whose width you want to adjust.
2. Right-click the selection and select **Column Width**.
3. In the Column Width dialog box, either:

   - Select the **Standard Width** check box to have Access change the width based on the default font (see the associated Tip).
   - Click **Best Fit** to change the column(s) width to be just wider than the widest content in each column.

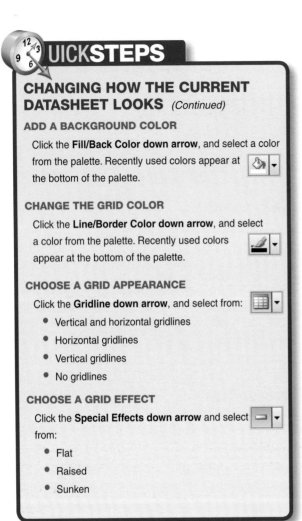

Move a Column

1. Click the column selector for the column you want to move.
2. Drag the column selector to the left or right to where you want the column located.
3. Release the mouse button when the heavy vertical line appears where you want the column located.

Rename a Column

1. Right-click the column selector of the column whose name you want to change, and select **Rename Column**.
2. Type a new name, and either press **ENTER** or click elsewhere in the datasheet.

Hide and Unhide Columns

Hidden columns provide a means to temporarily remove columns from view without deleting them or their contents. (See the QuickSteps, "Selecting Records, Fields, and Columns with the Mouse," for information selecting columns.)

Do either:

- To hide columns, select the column(s) to be hidden, right-click the selection, and choose **Hide**.
- To unhide columns, click **Format | Unhide Columns**, and select the check box next to hidden column(s) you want to show.

Lock and Unlock Columns

You can lock (or *freeze*) one or more columns to the leftmost side of the datasheet so they are visible no matter where in the datasheet you might be.

Do either:

- To lock columns, select the column(s) you want to lock, and click **Format | Freeze Columns**.
- To unlock columns, click **Format | Unfreeze All Columns**.

Figure 4-13: Most formatting changes you make on the Datasheet tab affect new datasheets only.

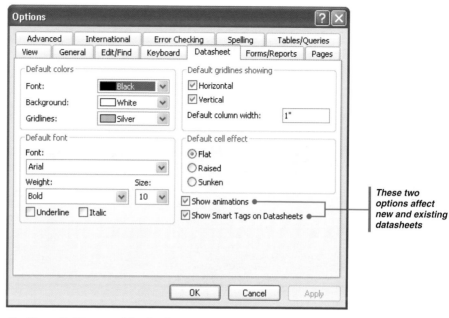

These two options affect new and existing datasheets

Adjust Row Height

You can adjust the height of all rows in the datasheet by using the mouse, by typing a precise value, or by choosing a default height. Do one of the following:

- To change row height with the mouse, point at the bottom border of a record selector. When the pointer changes to a cross with up and down arrowheads, drag the border up or down to the height you want.

- To change row height precisely, click **Format | Row Height**. In the Row Height dialog box, type a row height (12.75 is the default height for the default font), and click **OK**.

- To use the default row height, click **Format | Row Height**. In the Row Height dialog box, select the **Standard Height** check box, and click **OK**.

Chapter 5

Retrieving Information

A great deal of Access is geared toward getting data into tables. You learn how to create tables, set field properties, and how to enter the data. Those are all worthwhile and needed skills you need to develop, but the *value* of data lies in finding ways to extract from it just the information you want for a particular need. In this chapter you will learn how to organize data by sorting; how to filter data so you see only the fields you want; and how to create queries, which can do everything filters do and much more.

Sort Data

Sorting allows you to reorganize your data by taking values in one or more columns and placing their corresponding records in an ascending or descending order. There are no permanent changes made to the data—you can easily return your data to the view you started with.

Sort Records in a Datasheet

Typically, records are sorted sequentially by the primary key as they are entered. You can alter this *sort order* by choosing to sort all records based on the values in a different column, or even in multiple columns, as shown in Figure 5-1.

SORT ON ONE COLUMN

1. In the database whose data you want to sort, open the table in Datasheet view (see Chapter 4).

2. Click a value under the field name that you want to sort your data on.

3. On the Table Datasheet toolbar, either:

   - Click **Sort Ascending** to sort from smaller to larger numbers and from A to Z.

     –Or–

   - Click **Sort Descending** to sort from larger to smaller numbers and from Z to A.

4. When you close the datasheet, you will be asked if you want to change the design of the table. Clicking **Yes** will save the sort order. The next time you open the datasheet, the data will display with its new sort order.

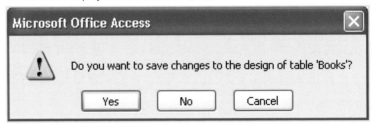

SORT ON MULTIPLE COLUMNS

You can sort on two or more columns by positioning them adjacent to one another in the datasheet, with the leftmost column being the one to be sorted first. The column directly to the right of the leftmost column will be sorted next, and so on, as shown in Figure 5-1.

TIP

To remove a sort (or filter), right-click the data and select **Remove Filter/Sort** from the context menu, or click **Records | Remove Filter/Sort**.

Sorting on multiple columns by moving columns into the sort precedence you want (or *simple* sort), sorts all columns by the same sort order you choose, ascending or descending. If you want some columns to be sorted ascending and some descending you, will need to use the Advanced Filter/Sort window to do a *complex* sort. See "Use Advanced Filters," later in the chapter.

1. In the database whose data you want to sort, open the table in Datasheet view (see Chapter 4).

2. Move the columns that you want to sort on so that they are adjacent, with the leftmost column as the one to be sorted first and the rightmost as the one to be sorted last (see Chapter 4 for information moving and selecting columns).

3. Select the columns you want sort on, and on the Table Datasheet toolbar, either:

   • Click **Sort Ascending** to sort from smaller to larger numbers and from A to Z.

   –Or–

   • Click **Sort Descending** to sort from larger to smaller numbers and from Z to A.

4. When you close the datasheet, you will be asked if you want to change the design of the table. Clicking **Yes** will save the sort order. The next time you open the datasheet, the data will display with its new sort order.

Records are first sorted by Category...

...then by Title within a Category

Books : Table

BkID	ISBN	Category	Title	Price
▶ 28	0688066631	Adventure	Whirlwind	$22.95
23	0671700553	Biography	Against the Grain	$19.95
15	0671691988	Biography	An American Life	$24.95
19	0553070118	Biography	Father Son & Co.	$22.95
22	0471568864	Biography	Hard Drive	$22.95
14	0345377702	Biography	Me	$5.99
31	0385182694	Biography	Overdrive	$16.95
2	1559582251	Business	Making of Microsoft	$12.30
24	0679505288	Business	The Rise & Fall of the DC10	$19.95

Figure 5-1: You can sort on multiple columns by moving them into a leftmost/first sorted to rightmost/last sorted arrangement.

Sort Records in a Form

You can sort records using a form in Form view and then move through them in the new sort order.

1. In the database whose data you want to sort, open the form in Form view (see Chapter 6 for information on working with forms).

2. Click the field in the form that you want to sort on.

3. On the Form View toolbar, either:

   • Click **Sort Ascending** to sort from smaller to larger numbers and from A to Z.

   –Or–

   • Click **Sort Descending** to sort from larger to smaller numbers and from Z to A.

Depending on your choice of sort order, you will see either the first or last record in the table or form, as shown in Figure 5-2.

Figure 5-2: Clicking the last name field and then clicking the Sort Descending button displays the record with "Vanderbilt" as the first record in the new sort order.

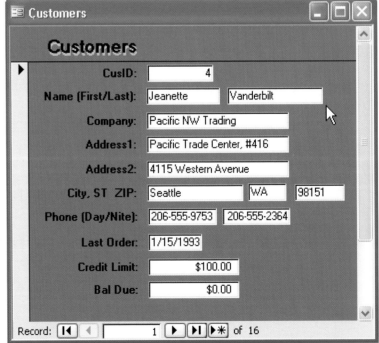

NOTE

You can filter records in a table datasheet/subdatasheet (see Chapters 3 and 4), form/subform (see Chapter 6), or query (see "Work with Queries," later in this chapter). The procedures, figures, and illustrations in this chapter use datasheets as the primary example object. The filtering techniques work similarly for each object.

TIP

All filters are "saved" with the datasheet or form in which they were created until they are replaced with a new filter. When you close the datasheet or form, you will be asked if you want save changes to the design of the object. Clicking **Yes** will allow you to reapply the filter the next time you open the object. Advanced filters can also be saved as a query and be run irrespective of subsequent filters you've created. See "Save an Advanced Filter," later in the chapter.

Filter Data

Filtering, by one of several methods, lets you focus on specific records you want to see while hiding from view the rest of the data in the datasheet. Setting up a filter can be as simple as selecting a value in a field (datasheet column) and clicking a button, or you can apply complex criteria to multiple columns and save the filter design as a *query* (working with queries is discussed later in the chapter). In a filter, you enter a value (and/or add *criteria*) in a field that you want to find in all other records that have the same value (or meet the criteria you set) in the same field. For example, you might want to find all salespersons that have the value "Washington" in their Territory field. You would filter on "Washington" in the Territory field, and only those records that satisfied that criteria would be displayed. The record for a salesperson named "Joe Washington" whose Territory is New York would not be displayed since "Washington," in this case, is not in the filtered field.

Filter by Selecting a Value

Filtering by selection is the easiest filter to perform, especially in small databases. The main stipulation to using this filter is that you are able to quickly locate the value on which the filter is based.

1. Open a table in Datasheet or Form view.

2. Select the value in the field that you want to filter on, as shown in Figure 5-3. What part of the value you select will determine the breadth and focus of the return you will get. Do one of the following:

   • Click a value (select no characters) or select the entire value to return records whose filtered field matches the entire value.

   • Select the first character(s) of a value to return records whose filtered field starts with the same character(s).

   • Select any character(s) to return records whose filtered field contains the selected character(s) in any part of the field contents.

QUICKSTEPS

CHOOSING A FILTER

The filter you choose will depend on the size of your data and the complexity of your filtering criteria. The main functionality for the filter types are:

- **Filter By Selection** lets you select a value in the datasheet or form.

- **Filter By Form** lets you select values from a drop-down list or enter your own.

- **Filter By Input** lets you type your criteria in a text box.

- **Filter Excluding Selection** lets you select a value in the datasheet or form, and displays all records that *don't* match the selected value.

- **Advanced Filter** lets you design the filter in a grid where you can sort the data, use operators and wildcard to set criteria, and save the filter as a query.

3. Click the **Filter By Selection** button on the Table Datasheet or Form View toolbar, or right-click the value and select **Filter By Selection** on the context menu. The filtered records are displayed. Contrast the filtered records to the unfiltered datasheet shown in Figure 5-3.

Figure 5-3: You can broaden or focus your filter by choosing what portion of the value is selected.

Filtering on "Co" in "Computer"…

…will return the records with "Computer" or "Cooking"

…but not those with "Children"

4. To remove the filter and return the data back to its pre-filtered state, click the **Remove Filter** button on the Table Datasheet or Form View toolbar, or right-click the object and select **Remove Filter/Sort** on the context menu.

Filter by Form

You can create a filter by choosing a value to filter on from a drop-down list of all values in the field, or you can type the value and/or add operators and wildcards. (See "Use Operators and Wildcards in Criteria," later in the chapter.)

1. Open a table in Datasheet or Form view.

2. Click **Filter By Form** on the Table Datasheet or Form View toolbar. You will see either:

   - A one-line blank record in Datasheet view.

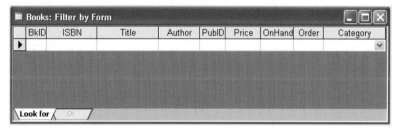

   –Or–

   - A blank set of fields in Form view.

3. Click the field you want to filter on. A down arrow will appear at the right end of the field, as shown in Figure 5-4. Do one of the following:

   - Click the **down arrow** and select the value you want to filter on from the drop-down list.

   - Type the value you want to filter on in the field.

   - Type operators and wildcards in addition to typed or selected values.

4. Click **Apply Filter** on the Table Datasheet or Form View toolbar.

5. To remove the filter and return the data back to its pre-filtered state, click the **Remove Filter** button on the Table Datasheet or Form View toolbar, or right-click the object and select **Remove Filter/Sort** on the context menu.

UICKSTEPS

DELETING OR REMOVING A FILTER

When you *delete* a filter, you permanently strike it from the object it's associated with. When you merely *remove* a filter, it can be reapplied. To re-create a deleted filter, you have to start from scratch.

REMOVE A FILTER

Click the **Remove Filter** button.

REAPPLY THE MOST RECENT FILTER

Click the **Apply Filter** button (same button as Remove Filter).

DELETE A FILTER

1. Open the datasheet or form that contains the filter you want to delete.

2. Click **Records | Filter | Advanced Filter/Sort** to display the advanced filter window.

3. Click **Clear Grid** on the Filter/Sort toolbar, or click **Edit | Clear Grid**.

4. Click **Apply Filter** on the Filter/Sort toolbar, or click **Filter | Apply Filter/Sort**.

Figure 5-4: You can select a value to filter on from a drop-down list, or you can type a value and other criteria.

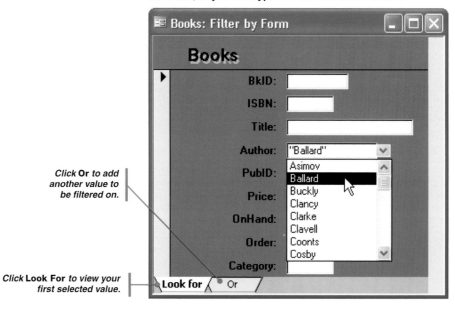

Click Or to add another value to be filtered on.

Click Look For to view your first selected value.

Filter for an Input

You can type a value, operators, and wildcards in a text box to quickly filter your data.

1. Right-click the field in Datasheet or Form view where you want to type a value or where you want to type a value along with criteria.

2. Type your value and criteria in the Filter For: text box.

3. Press **ENTER** when finished. The filtered records are displayed.

4. To remove the filter and return the data back to its pre-filtered state, click the **Remove Filter** button on the Table Datasheet or Form View toolbar, or right-click the object and select **Remove Filter/Sort** on the context menu.

Use Operators and Wildcards in Criteria

You can "juice up" how records are filtered by using *operators* and *wildcards*. These are symbols and other characters that tell the filter or query to return certain results. For example, if you use "12.95" in a Price field, the filter or query would return only those records that contained a $12.95 price. If you entered the greater-than-or-equal- to operator, ">=12.95" Access would return those records greater than or equal to $12.95.

USE COMPARISON OPERATORS

See Table 5-1 for a list and descriptions of common operators you can use to compare a value.

TABLE 5-1: COMPARISON OPERATORS

COMPARISON OPERATOR	DESCRIPTION
>	Greater than
>=	Greater than or equal to
<	Less than
<=	Less than or equal to
=	Equal to
<>	Not equal to
Between	The inclusive values between two values. (For example, "between 9 and 12" would return 9, 10, 11, and 12.)

TABLE 5-2:
ARITHMETIC OPERATORS

ARITHMETIC OPERATOR	DESCRIPTION
+	Addition
*	Multiplication
/	Division
-	Subtraction

TABLE 5-3: LOGICAL OPERATORS

LOGICAL OPERATOR	DESCRIPTION
and	Both values must be satisfied
or	Either value must be satisfied
not	The value is not satisfied

USE ARITHMETIC OPERATORS

See Table 5-2 for a list and descriptions of common operators you can use to calculate a value.

USE LOGICAL OPERATORS

See Table 5-3 for a list and descriptions of common operators you can use to apply logical comparisons.

USE WILDCARDS

Wildcards are characters that act as placeholders in expressions used in filters or queries when you are trying to find a particular word or string of characters and only know limited information about the value. Typically used in Text fields, you can often use them in other data types. Table 5-4 lists the most commonly used wildcards.

TIP

You can also use wildcards in the Find and Replace dialog boxes (click **Edit | Find** or **Edit | Replace**). See Chapter 4 for information on finding and replacing text in a table.

TABLE 5-4:
WILDCARDS

WILDCARD	DESCRIPTION
*	Used as a placeholder for all characters that occupies the space. For example, filtering on a value of *son would return values that started with any characters as long as they ended in "son," such as Robertson and comparison.
?	Used as a placeholder for a single character. For example, filtering on a value of r??der would return values that contained any characters in the second and third positions, such as reader and Ridder.
[ ]	Returns values that match any characters you type between the brackets. For example, the[mr]e would return there and theme, but not Thebe.
!	Returns values that don't match the characters you type between brackets. For example, the[!mr]e would return Thebe, but not there or theme.
-	Returns values that match a range of characters between brackets. For example, the[m-z]e would return there and theme, but not Thebe.
#	Used as a placeholder, similar to ?, but used to replace a single numeric character.

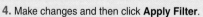

QUICKSTEPS

RUNNING AND MODIFYING A SAVED ADVANCED FILTER

See "Work with Queries" for more information on using queries to extract and modify records.

RUN A SAVED ADVANCED FILTER

1. Open the database that contains the query/ advanced filter.

2. In the Database window, select **Queries**, and double-click the name of the query/advanced filter.

MODIFY A SAVED ADVANCED FILTER

1. Open the database that contains the query/ advanced filter.

2. Open the table from where the advanced filter was saved, and click **Records | Filter | Advanced Filter/ Sort**.

3. Click the **Load From Query** button on the Filter/Sort toolbar to display the Applicable Filter dialog box. Choose a filter and click **OK**. The filter opens in the advanced filter window.

4. Make changes and then click **Apply Filter**.

Use Advanced Filters

Advanced filters allow you to easily use multiple criteria in multiple fields (columns) to find and sort records.

You can also use *expressions* to set up criteria. Expressions used in filters are typically short combinations of values, operators, wildcards, and other terms that return a value.

CREATE AN ADVANCED FILTER

1. Open a table in Datasheet or Form view.

2. Click **Records | Filter | Advanced Filter/Sort**. The advanced filter window opens.

3. Click the **Field down arrow** in the leftmost column of the grid in the lower half of window. Select the first field that you want to search. (See "Work in the Grid" later in this chapter for other ways to choose the field you want.)

4. If you want to sort your results, click inside the Sort field and open its drop-down menu. Select the sort order you want.

5. In the Criteria field, type the first criteria you want to apply in the current field. (See "Use Operators and Wildcards in Criteria," earlier in the chapter.)

6. Type a second criteria, as necessary, in the "or" field. Records that satisfy either condition will be returned. Repeat for any other criteria you want to add.

7. Repeat steps 3-6 to apply criteria in multiple fields, as shown in Figure 5-5.

8. Click **Apply Filter** on the Filter/Sort toolbar to display the results.

TIP

To clear any existing criteria in the grid, click the **Clear Grid** button on the Filter/Sort toolbar; or right-click an area of the window outside the grid, and select **Clear Grid**.

NOTE

To help you set up expressions, Access has an Expression Builder tool that allows you to build the expression from lists and buttons. Right-click a criteria field and select **Build** to display the Expression Builder window. See the QuickSteps, "Using the Expression Builder," later in the chapter.

Figure 5-5: The advanced filter window lets you set up complex filters and sort the results.

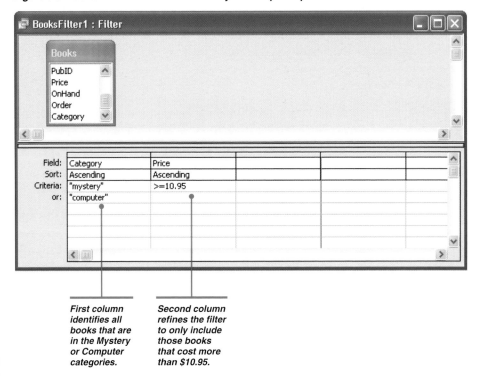

First column identifies all books that are in the Mystery or Computer categories.

Second column refines the filter to only include those books that cost more than $10.95.

SAVE AN ADVANCED FILTER

You can save a filter you set up in the advanced filter window as a query and run it at a future time.

1. Set up the filter in the advanced filter window.

2. Prior to applying the filter, click the **Save As Query** button on the Filter/Sort toolbar.

3. In the Save As Query dialog box, type a name for the query. Click **OK**.

NOTE

Queries are opened, designed, and created from commands or buttons in the Queries object category in the Database window. To *open* a query means to display the result of the query in a datasheet; to *design* a query means to open a selected query in Design view; and to create a *new* query means to choose from a list what type of query you want to create.

Work with Queries

Queries offer the most powerful and flexible way to work with the data in your database. They allow you to retrieve, change, add to, and analyze data from one or more tables or queries. Queries respond to the criteria you set and display the resultant data in a datasheet. The *Select* queries family—such as Simple, Parameter, Find Duplicates, and Find Unmatched—do so without changing any underlining data. *Action* queries (such as Make-Table, Update, Append, and Delete) cause the underlying to data to change. You can also analyze data by using Crosstab queries (see Chapter 10 for information on Crosstab queries).

Create a Simple Query with a Wizard

The easiest way to create a Select query is let Access guide you using the Simple Query wizard. The operant word in the wizard name is "Simple." The wizard doesn't try to help you establish criteria, other than letting you choose what fields (columns) you want to include. After finishing the query, you will most likely need to modify the design (see the following section, "Modify a Query").

1. Open the database in which you want to create the query.

2. In the Database window, click **Queries** and then click **New** on the Database window toolbar.

3. In the New Query dialog box, select **Simple Query Wizard**, and click **OK**.

TIP

You can identify many queries by their icons in the Database window (and the type of query name appears in the query Design view window title bar). For example, Select queries show overlapping datasheets, all action queries show an exclamation point (!) along with a specific identifier (Append queries add a cross, Delete queries add an X, Make-Table queries add a table, and Update queries add a wand), and Crosstab queries show a PivotTable.

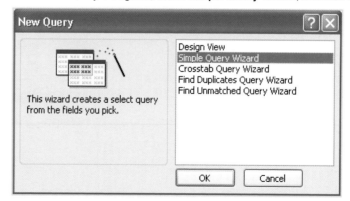

4. In the first dialog box of the Simple Query Wizard, shown in Figure 5-6, click the **Tables/Queries down arrow** and choose the table or query from where you first want to select the fields that will appear in your query results.

5. Move the fields you want from the Available Fields to the Selected Fields list box by either double-clicking the fields you want or by using the select/remove buttons between the two list boxes to add or remove fields.

6. Repeat Steps 4 and 5 if you want to include fields from other tables or queries. Click **Next** when finished adding fields.

7. In the Finish Line flag dialog box, type a title/name for the query and choose whether to open (run) the query as is or to modify its design. If you need additional help, select the **Display Help On Working With The Query** check box. Click **Finish** when done. Depending on the choice you selected, the new query will appear as a datasheet with the resultant fields you

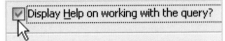

selected earlier in the wizard, or it will open in *Design view*, ready for adding criteria and other changes. In either case, the new query will be listed under Queries in the Database window.

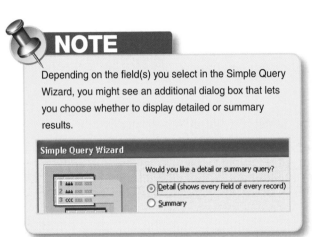

NOTE

Depending on the field(s) you select in the Simple Query Wizard, you might see an additional dialog box that lets you choose whether to display detailed or summary results.

Figure 5-6: The Simple Query Wizard provides listing of tables and queries from which you can choose fields to include in your query.

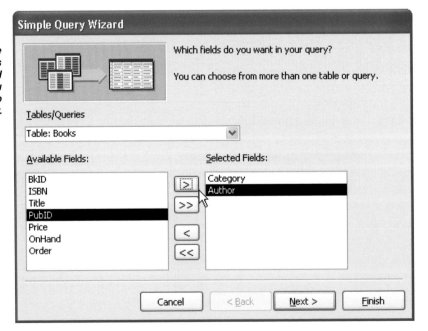

Create or Modify a Query in Design View

Queries use a Design view window, as shown in Figure 5-7, where you can modify an existing query (for example, a query created by using the Simple Query Wizard) or start one from scratch.

Figure 5-7: The query Design view window provides everything you need to set up or change a query.

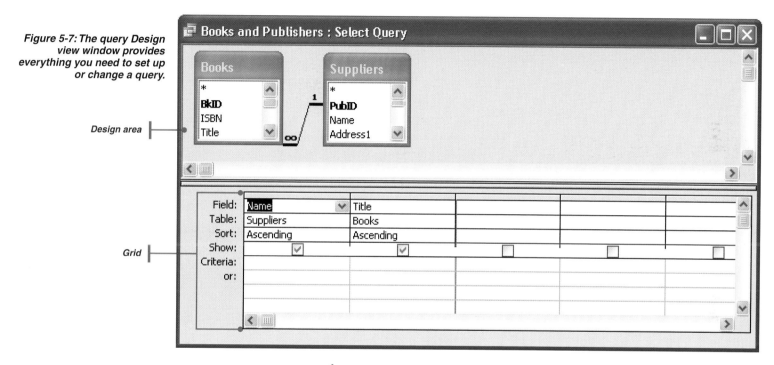

1. Select **Queries** in the Database window.

2. Either:

   - Click **New** on the toolbar and double-click **Design View** in the New Query dialog box to open a blank Design view window.

   –Or–

   - Double-click an existing query to open the query in Design view.

CAUTION

If you add multiple tables to a query, they may not function as designed unless they have a *relationship*. Right-click a blank portion of the design area, and select **Relationships** from the context menu to view the current related tables (see Chapter 2 for information on joining tables).

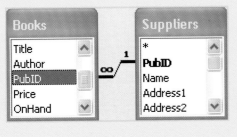

WORK IN THE DESIGN AREA

The top portion, or *design area*, of the query Design view window displays the fields, tables, and queries that you want the query to use in performing the actions you ask of it. (Existing queries will show their associated tables and queries; new queries will show a blank palette.)

1. Click **Show Table** on the Query Design toolbar to display the Show Table dialog box, shown in Figure 5-8. Choose which tables and/or queries you want to include (press **CTRL** while clicking objects to select multiple objects).

2. Click **OK**. The objects are added to the design area.

3. Click the **Query Type down arrow** on the Query Design toolbar and select the query you want. Depending on your selection, you will see a tailored grid at the bottom of the window and/or be presented with a dialog box requesting more information from you.

4. To remove an object from the design area, right-click the object and select **Remove Table**.

Figure 5-8: Add tables and queries to the design area from the Show Table dialog box.

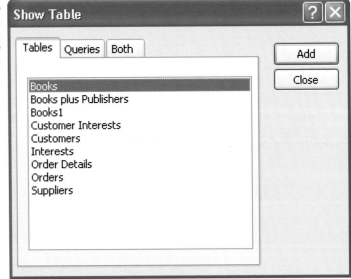

WORK IN THE GRID

The lower portion of the query Design view window, or *grid*, contains columns that you set up, on a field-by-field basis, using the fields from the tables and queries in the design area. Each column has several parameters you can apply to fully build your query.

1. Add the first (or only) field to the leftmost column by locating it in the table or query in the design area and dragging it into the field labeled Field. You can also click the field in the grid, open its drop-down list, and select the field you want.

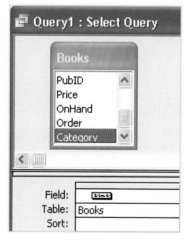

2. If you want to sort your results, click the field labeled Sort, open its drop-down menu, and select the sort order you want.

3. Select the **Show** check box if you want the values from this field to display after the query is run.

4. Type expressions, values, or other criteria in the Criteria field; or click **Build** on the Query Design toolbar to have the Expression Builder help you construct an expression (see the QuickSteps, "Using the Expression Builder," later in the chapter).

5. Repeat Steps 1-4 for other fields you want to include in the query.

VIEW THE QUERY RESULTS

In query Design view, click **Run** on the Query Design toolbar. Depending on the query type you are using, you will either see the results displayed in a datasheet or you will need to supply additional criteria in a dialog box.

SAVE A QUERY

1. Do one of the following:

   • Click **Save** on the Query Design toolbar.

   • Click **Close** in the Design view window.

   • Run the query, click **Close** in the datasheet window, and click **Yes** in the dialog box that asks if you want to save the query.

2. Type a name in the Save As dialog box, and click **OK**. The query will be displayed under Queries in the Database window.

STOP A QUERY

Press **CTRL+BREAK**.

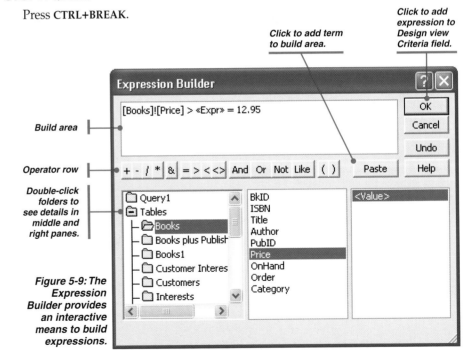

Click to add term to build area.

Click to add expression to Design view Criteria field.

Build area

Operator row

Double-click folders to see details in middle and right panes.

Figure 5-9: The Expression Builder provides an interactive means to build expressions.

USING THE EXPRESSION BUILDER

The Expression Builder, shown in Figure 5-9, provides listings and buttons for the expression terms from which you select to build your own expression.

CREATE OR EDIT AN EXPRESSION

Do either:

- In query Design view or in an advanced filter, right-click a Criteria field and select **Build**.

- In query Design view, click **Build** on the Query Design toolbar.

ADD AN EXPRESSION TERM

1. Double-click the folders containing database objects, functions, constants, operators and common expressions you want in the left, and possibly middle, pane to see their details in the other pane(s) to the right.

2. Double-click the term you want in the middle or right pane, or click **Paste**. The term is added to the build area at the top of the dialog box.

3. Repeat Steps 1 and 2 to add other terms to the expression.

ADD OPERATORS

Click your insertion point in the build area where you want the operator added. Do either:

- Click the applicable button from the center row.

- Double-click **Operators** in the left pane, select a category in the middle pane, and double-click the operator in the right pane.

ADD VALUES

1. Click your insertion point in the build area where you want the value added, or typically, the Expression Builder will correctly set up the build area expression for you after inserting an operator.

2. Type the value.

ADD THE EXPRESSION TO THE CRITERIA FIELD

Click **OK** in the Expression Builder dialog box.

Set Query Properties

You can fine-tune several characteristics of a query by changing the attributes of its properties, as shown in Figure 5-10.

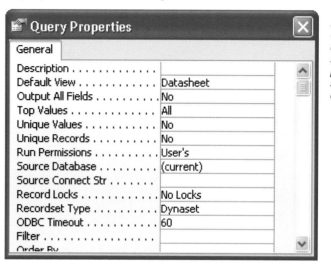

Figure 5-10: The Queries Properties dialog box lists several query properties whose settings can be chosen or modified.

OPEN THE QUERY PROPERTIES DIALOG BOX

Open the query in Design view, and do one of the following:

- Click **Properties** on the Query Design toolbar.

- Right-click the query Design view window and select **Properties** from the context menu.

- Press **ALT+ENTER**.

SET OR MODIFY A PROPERTY

Click the box to the right of the property you want to set or change. Depending on the property, either:

- Type the setting you want to add or change.

  –Or–

- Click the **down arrow** and select the setting from the drop-down list.

TIP

You can cycle through the options available to a property (for those that have options) by double-clicking the property name.

NOTE

If you right-click a table or query in the design area and select **Properties**, you will see Field List Properties instead of the Query Properties dialog box.

LEARN ABOUT A PROPERTY

1. Click the box to the right of the property you want to learn about.

2. Press **F1**. A Property data sheet displays, providing a description of the property and information on its settings, as shown in Figure 5-11.

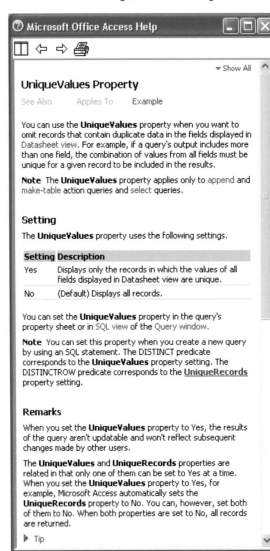

Figure 5-11: Detailed information about properties and their settings are readily available.

Chapter 6
Creating Forms and Using Controls

This chapter explains how to create a new form by using the Form Wizard and by creating one in Design view. You will then learn how to modify the form design to meet your needs and how to choose the appropriate controls and set their properties.

Create Forms

Access forms have many uses. Mainly used for data entry and viewing, they are also utilized as user-interactive elements that offer additional choices or request additional information.

You have more than one way to create a new form: by using the Form Wizard or by starting from scratch in the form Design view. Either way, you have complete flexibility with respect to the final appearance and behavior of the form, which will depend on your ultimate use for the form.

CREATING A FORM USING AUTOFORM

START AN AUTOFORM FROM THE DATABASE WINDOW

1. In the Database window, select the table or query you want to use in the form.

2. Click the **New Object down arrow** on the Database toolbar.

3. Select **AutoForm**.

START AN AUTOFORM WITH AN OPEN TABLE OR QUERY

1. With the table or query open in Datasheet view, click the **New Object down arrow** on the toolbar.

2. Select **Form**.

3. Select the type of AutoForm you want.

4. Click **OK**.

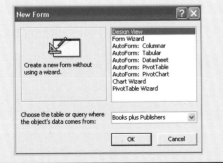

Get a Head Start with the Form Wizard

The quickest way to start a new form is with the Form Wizard.

1. To start the Form Wizard, either:

- Select **Tables** or **Queries** in the Objects pane of the Database window, click the **New Object down arrow**, and select **Form**.

–Or–

- Click **Forms** in the Objects pane of the Database window, and click **New**.

2. Choose **Form Wizard** in the New Form dialog box, as shown in Figure 6-1.

3. Select the table or query you want as the basis for the form.

4. Click **OK**.

Figure 6-1: You can choose from several methods when you create a new form.

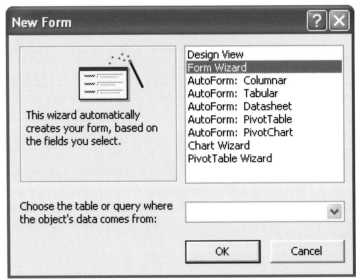

The fields appear in the form in the same order as in the underlying table or query.

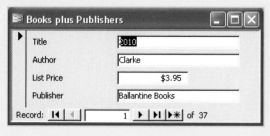

The Columnar style places all fields in one or more columns. The Tabular style places all data for each record in rows across the screen. The Datasheet style is the same as a table Datasheet view. The PivotTable and PivotChart styles are used to summarize and analyze data in charts and graphs.

If you create an AutoForm with the table or query open in Design view, you won't be able to view the form in Form view until you have closed the table or query.

SELECT THE FIELDS FOR THE FORM

1. In the Form Wizard dialog box, shown in Figure 6-2, do one or more of the following:

    ● To add all available fields, click the **double right arrow**.

    ● To select each field individually, click the **single right arrow**.

    ● To remove a field from the Selected Fields list, click the **single left arrow**.

    ● To remove all the fields from the Selected Fields list, click the **double left arrow**.

2. When you are satisfied with the field list and the order of the fields within the list, click **Next**.

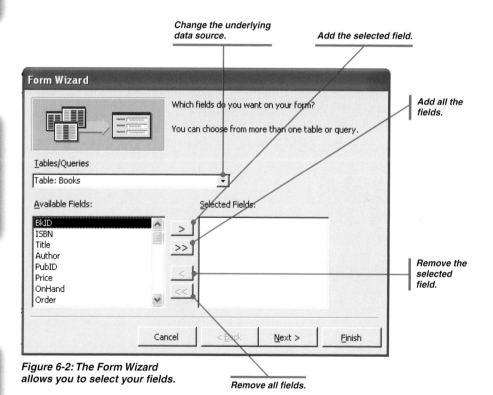

Figure 6-2: The Form Wizard allows you to select your fields.

ESTABLISH THE LAYOUT AND STYLE OF THE FORM

The next two Form Wizard dialog boxes offer you choices of layout (see Figure 6-3) and style (see Figure 6-4).

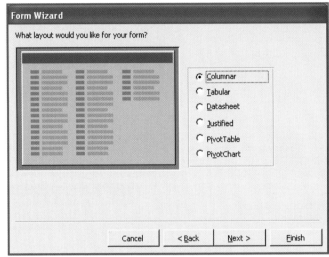

Figure 6-3: Choose an appropriate style for the new form.

1. Select each style and look at the sample pane.

2. Choose the one you want, and click **Next**.

3. Choose an appropriate style, and click **Next**.

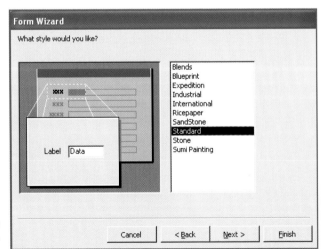

Figure 6-4: Choose the new form style.

TITLE THE FORM AND CHOOSE THE FINISHED VIEW

1. Enter the form name in the last dialog box.

2. You have two options. Either:

   ● Open the form in Form view to see the results with the data (the default choice).

   –Or–

   ● Go directly to Design view to make changes in the form.

3. Click **Finish**. The completed form resembles Figure 6-5.

Figure 6-5: View the finished form in Form view.

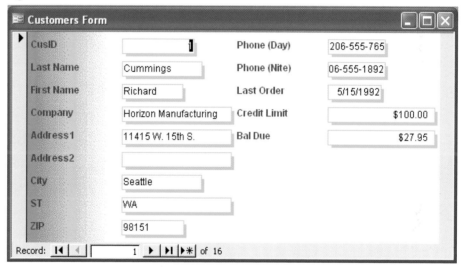

QUICKSTEPS

CREATING A TWO-TABLE FORM

You can choose fields from more than one table (they need to be related tables).

1. Click **Forms** in the Objects pane of the Database window.

2. Double-click **Create Form By Using Wizard**.

3. Click the **Tables/Queries down arrow**, and select the main table from the Tables/Queries list.

4. Double-click each field you want. The fields move to the Selected Fields list box.

5. Repeat Step 3 and select the related table from the Tables/Queries list.

6. Select the fields from that table.

7. Click **Finish**, or click **Next** to continue the wizard.

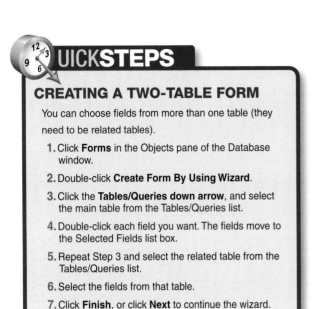

Create a Form in Design View

You have several ways to begin the design of a new form without the help of the Form Wizard. You also have the option of choosing a table or query as the basis for the new form, or creating a form not linked to existing data. A switchboard is an example of a form that doesn't rely on data—instead, it offers a choice of actions.

Figure 6-6: Start a new form design from the Forms area of the Database window.

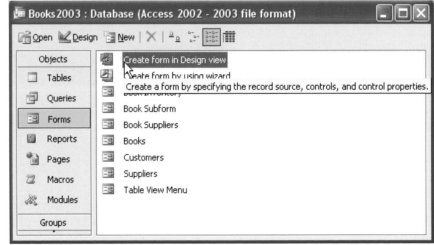

1. Click **Forms** on the Database window to open the form area, as shown in Figure 6-6.

2. Do one of the following:

   - Double-click **Create Form In Design View**.

   - Click **New and click OK in the New Form dialog box**.

   - Click **Insert | Form** on the Access menu bar.

   - Click the **New Object down arrow** on the toolbar, and choose **Form.** Then click **OK**.

3. Choose **Design View** in the New Form dialog box.

4. Click the **down arrow** and choose a table or query to use as the basis for the form.

5. Click **OK**.

NOTE

Choosing Create A Form In Design view opens a blank form design. If you start from the New button, with the Insert menu or the New Object button, you will see the New Form dialog box displayed.

TIP

Rulers are handy. If you don't see them, click **View | Ruler**.

TIP

If you don't see the Formatting or Form Design toolbars, right-click any blank space in the visible toolbar, and select the toolbar(s) you want from the list.

Figure 6-7 shows the blank form design with the list of fields from the table or query you chose as the basis for the form.

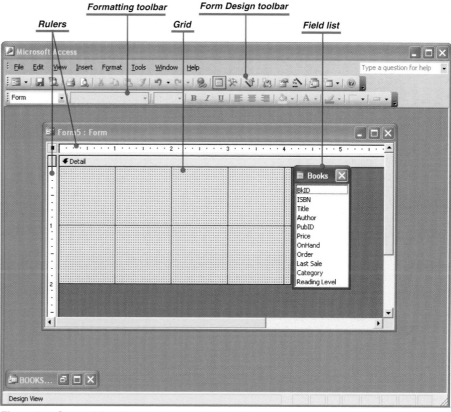

Figure 6-7: Start adding fields to the new form design.

TIP

If the fields do not appear in the order you want in the form, drag them one at a time from the field list to the form design grid.

TIP

If you don't see the field list in the form design window, click the **Field List** button on the Form Design toolbar.

Add Fields

The first step in creating a form for showing data is to add the fields to the design.

1. Add fields from the list to the form by using one of the following methods (see Figure 6-8):

Figure 6-8: You decide where to place your fields in the form design.

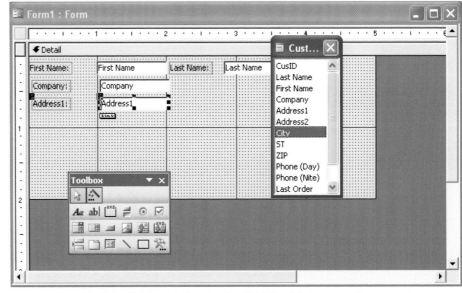

- **To add all the fields**, double-click the **field list title bar**, and then drag the group to the form. They will appear in a column in the form.

- **To add one field**, drag its field name from the list to the design grid.

- **To add a contiguous group of fields**, click the first field name, press and hold **SHIFT**, and click the last field name in the group. Then drag the group to the form design.

- **To add a group of dispersed field names**, press and hold **CTRL** while clicking each field name. Then drag the group to the form design.

2. Click the **field move handle** to drag each field to the desired location.

3. Click the **Close** button to close the field list.

Explore the Toolbox Tools

The toolbox displays buttons for the commonly used form and report controls. The toolbox is actually a floating toolbar.

1. Open the toolbox using one of the following methods:
   - Click the **Toolbox** button on the Design toolbar.
   - Click **View | Toolbox**.
   - Right-click in the visible toolbar, and click **Toolbox**.

2. Move the mouse pointer over the buttons on the toolbox to view the ScreenTips about the controls you can add to the form.

3. Make sure the Select Objects button is selected (double-click it to "lock" it down).

4. Also, make sure the Control Wizards button is selected, so that you will have the help of the many Control Wizards that are available.

Table 6-1 lists and describes the controls that are most commonly used in forms.

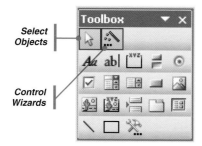

Select Objects

Control Wizards

TABLE 6-1: CONTROLS COMMONLY USED IN FORM DESIGN

CONTROL NAME	DESCRIPTION
Label	A block of text such as a title, a description, or instructions for the user
Text Box	A control that displays the values stored in fields in the underlying table or query, including calculated fields
Option Group	A set of mutually exclusive options within a frame (can contain toggle buttons, option buttons or check boxes)
Toggle Button	A button that shows an on or off position
Option Button	A control that displays a Yes/No value
Check Box	A control that specifies a Yes/No value from the underlying record source
Combo Box	A control that displays a drop-down list of values with a text box for data entry
List Box	A control that displays list of choices for user interaction (can represent a field value or search criteria)
Command Button	A button that starts an action—such as opening a report, running a macro, or initializing a VBA procedure
Image	An unbound picture, such as a company logo, that has no ties to the underlying data in the form

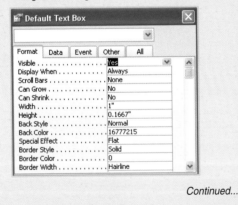
Modify the Form Design

When you have completed the form design—either with the help of the Form Wizard or on your own—you can still make changes. Forms have many properties that determine their appearance and behavior.

1. Open the form in Design view.

2. Click the **Properties** button.

3. Click the **Format** tab. Figure 6-9 shows a partial list of the format properties you can set for the form. Other tabs in the property sheet offer data, event, and other properties.

Figure 6-9: Set the form properties with the Form property sheet.

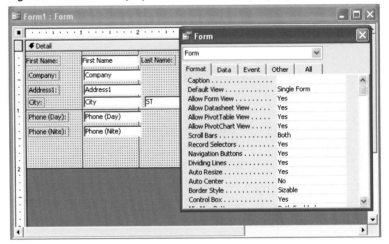

4. Click the **down-arrow** next to a property to see a list of choices.

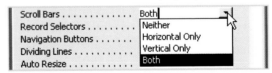

5. Select the property, and enter a value or select from the list of options.

6. Click another tab to change those properties.

7. When you have finished, close the property sheet, and click the **View** button or click **View | Form**.

USING THE TOOLBOX *(Continued)*

LOOK AT MORE TOOLS

Click the **More Controls** button to see a long list of available objects.

> :-) VideoSoft FlexArray Control
> :-) VideoSoft FlexString Control
> ACApptTypeCombo Class
> ACCalendarDCtrl Class
> ACCalendarListCtrl Class
> ACColorPick Class
> ACDayBoxViewCtrl Class
> ACEventConflictCtrl Class
> ACMonthViewCtrl Class
> ACMPickerCtrl Class
> Acrobat Control for ActiveX
> ActionBvr Class
> ActiveMovieControl Object

MOVE, RESIZE, AND DOCK THE TOOLBOX

- Click the **toolbox title bar** to drag it around the screen. Dragging it to the top, bottom, or to one side of the window will dock it.

- Drag the **toolbox borders** to change the height and width of the floating toolbox.

- Click the **Close** button to remove the toolbox from the screen.

TIP

If the window containing the form in Form view is not maximized and shows a lot of blank space around it, you can resize the window to fit the form by clicking **Window | Size to Fit Form**. Click **Save** to keep the new dimensions.

FORMAT A FORM

The Formatting toolbar offers shortcuts for specifying the appearance of the controls in the form. Rest the mouse pointer on a button to see its name.

The Format tab of the property sheet, as mentioned in the previous section, offers additional format settings for the form, form sections, and controls.

If you have created a form with the Form Wizard, you know that you had choices of layout and style. After you have finished the form design, you can still change the form style with AutoFormat.

1. Open the form in Design view.

2. Click **AutoFormat** on the Form Design toolbar, or click **Format | AutoFormat**.

3. In the AutoFormat dialog box, shown in Figure 6-10, select the style you want.

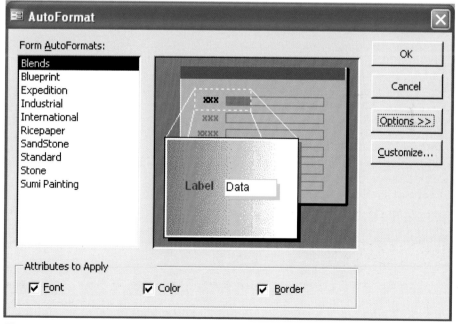

Figure 6-10: Change the form style with AutoFormat.

4. Click **Options** to open the Attributes to Apply pane, and select the elements you want affected by the new style: font, color, or border.

5. Click **OK**.

ADD A FORM HEADER AND FOOTER

Form headers can be useful to contain a form title, the current date, or some explanatory text. You can also place summary or other information in a form footer.

If you use both a header and footer, they need not have the same properties. You can give each a unique appearance.

To add a form header and footer, and to place the form title in the header:

1. Open the form in Design view.

2. Click **View | Header/Footer**.

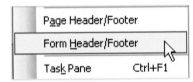

3. Click the **Toolbox** button.

4. Click the **Label** control tool.

5. Click inside the form header section, and type the title for the form.

To change the title appearance:

1. Click outside the label box, and then click it again to select the control.

2. Use the Formatting toolbar to change the font, size, bold/italic, and other format features. (You might need to increase the size of the control to accommodate an increased font size.)

NOTE

If you want to create your own customized format, click **Customize**.

NOTE

When you use the View menu to add a form header, both the header and footer are added to the design. If you have no use for the footer, you can drag the bottom form border up to reduce the section height to zero.

QUICKSTEPS

CHOOSING THE CONTROL TYPE

YES/NO BUTTONS

All Yes/No button controls do the same thing: they return a Yes or No value. All you need to do is determine their appearance:

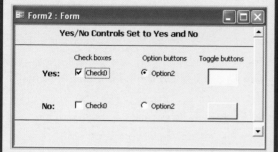

OPTION GROUPS

An option group control combines a set of Yes/No controls in a group within a frame. When the user selects one of the options, that value is stored in the field associated with the option group control. Further action depends on the value selected. For example, which report to print.

The Option Group Wizard helps you create an option group.

COMBO AND LIST BOXES

Combo boxes and list boxes are both bound to the underlying table data. The only difference between them is the amount of space they take up in the form.

- A **list box** displays a number of values in the field. How many values depends on the height of the control you draw in the design. If not all values fit in the box, a scroll bar is added.

- A **combo box** displays a single value with a down arrow that expands the list. Again, if there are more values than fit in the drop-down list, a scroll bar is added.

SELECT A FORM SECTION

Before you can work on a particular section of a form (or report), you need to select it. To select the form itself, do one of the following:

- If you see the rulers, click the **form selector** (the small square at the intersection of the horizontal and vertical rulers).

- Click **Edit | Select Form**.

- Click anywhere in the background outside the form design.

The form selector shows a small black square when the form is selected. The form header, footer, and detail sections also have selectors at the intersection of the section bar and the vertical ruler.

Use Controls

Form (and report) designs include two types of controls:

- **Bound** controls contain data stored directly in an Access table. For example, text boxes, combo, and list boxes are bound controls.

- **Unbound** controls are design elements unrelated to table data. For example, labels, command buttons, images, lines, and rectangles are unbound controls. These are discussed in the next section, "Add Unbound Controls."

Add Bound Controls

You can set up bound controls from a wizard or manually using the field list.

1. The easiest way to add table or query data to the design is to use the field list as described in "Add Fields," earlier in this chapter. To add other types of controls, use the toolbox. The form must be in Design view to add controls and make other design changes. Click the button for the control you want in the toolbox.

2. Click in the form design where you want the control. You may be asked to draw a rectangle for placing and sizing the control, depending on the type of control. A control wizard may also open offering help with the control.

Figure 6-11: Start a combo box with the help of a wizard.

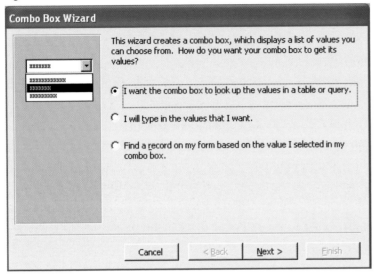

ADD A COMBO BOX CONTROL WITH THE WIZARD

Control Wizards are available for many of the control types. For example, you can add a combo box control that shows a list of book subject matter.

1. Click the **Toolbox** button.

2. Make sure the Controls Wizard button is selected, and then click the **Combo Box** tool.

3. Click in the form design where you want to place the combo box. Figure 6-11 shows the first Combo Box Wizard dialog box.

4. Choose **I Want The Combo Box To Look Up The Values In A Table Or Query**, and click Next.

5. Select the fields you want to see in the list, and click **Next**.

6. Drag the **right edge of the column border** to adjust the column widths to fit the field values, as shown in Figure 6-12, and choose whether to show or hide the primary key field. Click **Next**.

7. Choose **Store That Value In This Field**, and click Next.

8. If desired, enter a label for the combo box control in the text box at the top of the dialog box to replace the default label, and click **Finish**. Then switch to Form view to see the new combo box control.

Figure 6-12: Adjust the column width to fit its contents.

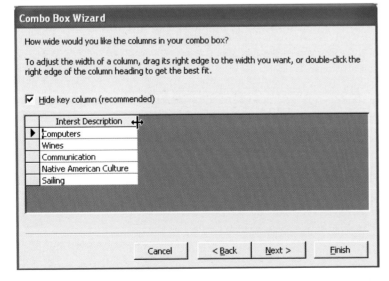

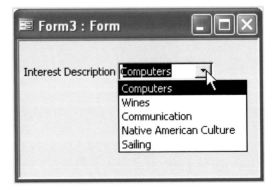

ADD A CALCULATED CONTROL

Calculated controls combine values from several text, number, currency, or date fields that are included in the underlying table or query. A calculated control is a text box control whose Control Source property is set to an expression. Here are some examples:

- **=[price]*[onhand]** displays the total value of the books of each title in the inventory.
- **=[Expiration Date]-Date()** displays the number of days until the expiration date.
- **=[First Name] & " " &[Last Name]** displays both the first name and last name with a space between.

Depending on the data type of the calculated control, you may need to change some of its formatting properties. For example, if the result is a currency field, you will want to see a dollar sign. If you want to see the result in a different font or in boldface, change those properties after creating the calculated control.

To add a calculated control:

1. Click the **Text Box** tool in the toolbox.
2. Click in the form design where you want the new control.
3. Click **Properties** and click the **Data** tab.
4. Select **Control Source** and enter the expression you want.
5. Click the **Format** tab to set the formatting properties that suit your needs, such as formatting currency or fonts.

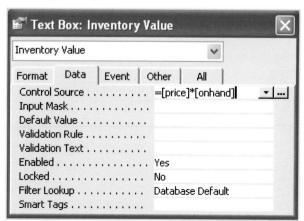

6. Select the label of your new text box, and enter **Value on Hand** in the Caption property box.

7. Click **Save** and switch to Form view to see the results.

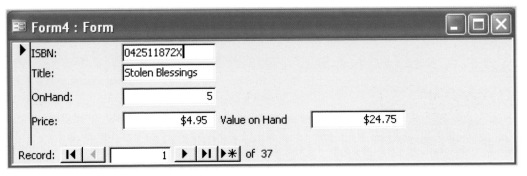

ADD A YES/NO CONTROL OR OPTION GROUP

Yes/No controls—such as toggle buttons, check boxes, and option buttons—can appear on a form as single controls or as part of an Option Group control. When you select or clear one of these buttons, the Yes or No value is displayed in the underlying table or query. The way it is displayed depends on the format property set in the table design.

To add one of the Yes/No controls to the form, click the control tool in the toolbox and click in the form design where you want the control.

Check boxes and option buttons include a generic label, while the toggle buttons show no label or image. To change a label, do the following:

1. Select the control label (not the Yes/No control itself), and click **Properties**.

2. Click the **Format** tab, and enter the desired text in the **Caption** property text box.

3. Switch to Form view to see the results.

Yes/No controls can be grouped within an Option Group that offers a list of mutually exclusive alternatives. The control itself is the frame around the Yes/No controls. The Option Group Wizard is on hand to guide you through adding an Option Group. Figure 6-13 shows an example of an option group from which you can choose a book category.

Add Unbound Controls

Unbound controls can be used to improve the appearance of the form and add some user interfacing tools, such as command buttons. You can also add the current date, time, and images to the form.

ADD A COMMAND BUTTON

Command buttons are true user interactive tools. For example, you can add a command button that opens or closes a form, moves to the next or to a new record, or deletes the current record. Through the Command Button Wizard, you can create over 30 different types of command buttons.

To add a command button that moves to the next record in Form view, open the form in Design view and do the following:

1. Make sure the Control Wizard's button is turned on the toolbox, and then click the **Command Button** tool.

2. Click in the form design where you want to place the button. Figure 6-14 shows the first Command Button Wizard dialog box, with the categories of commands in the left pane and groups of related individual commands in the right pane. The Sample pane displays the button's default image.

Figure 6-13: This option group offers a choice of literary interests.

NOTE

Select each of the categories to see what actions they offer.

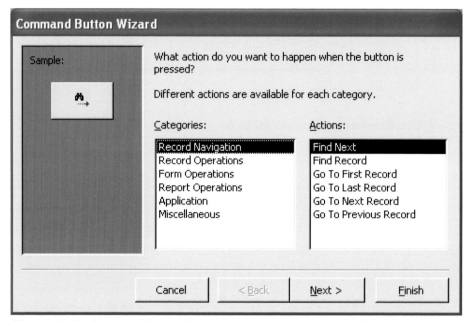

Figure 6-14: The Command Button Wizard allows you to create over 30 different types of commands.

3. In the left pane, choose the **Record Navigation** category.

4. Select **Go To Next Record** in the Actions pane. Click **Next**.

5. In the next dialog box, the Wizard lets you choose between text and a picture to show on the button. Do one of the following:

- Accept the default name.

- Enter a different name in the text box.

NOTE

If you choose an action such as open another form or preview a report, the Wizard will ask for the name of the form or report.

- Choose **Picture** and accept the default picture.

- Click **Show All Pictures** and choose another image from a list that includes all the Access icons.

6. Click **Next**.

7. When you are ready, click **Finish**

Figure 6-15: Select the appropriate date and time formats for the form.

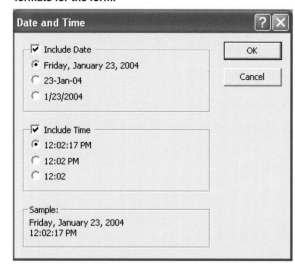

INSERT DATE AND TIME CONTROLS

Once you have the basic data-related controls in the form or report, you can add some special controls such as the current date and time, or an image.

To add the date and time:

1. Click **Insert | Date and Time**.

2. In the Date and Time dialog box, as shown in Figure 6-15, choose a date format.

3. If you want to include the time, select **Include Time** and choose a time format.

4. Click **OK**.

If the form includes a header section, the date/time control appears in the upper-left corner of the header. If not, it goes in the detail section.

INSERT IMAGE CONTROLS

You can add image controls to display a picture or other image. To add an image:

1. Either:

   - Click the **Image** toolbox button and draw a frame in the form design.

     –Or–

   - Click **Insert | Picture**.

2. In the Insert Picture dialog box, use the Look In box to locate the folder with the picture you want to add.

3. Click the **Views down arrow** and choose **Preview** so you can look at the pictures before choosing one, as shown in Figure 6-16.

4. After viewing the selections, select the picture you want to add, and click **OK**.

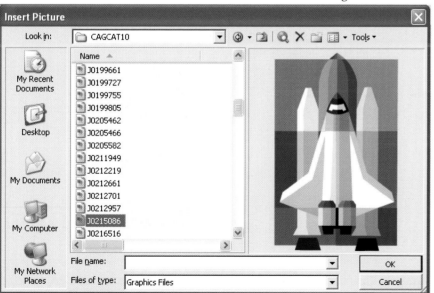

Figure 6-16: The Insert Picture dialog box lets you preview graphic files before placing them.

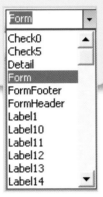
Copy or Delete a Control

After you have built a control and have set its special properties, you can create copies of it to add to the form design.

1. Click the control itself, not the label.

2. Do one of the following:

- Right-click and choose **Copy**, then right-click again and choose **Paste**.
- Right-click and choose **Copy**, then click the **Paste** toolbar button.
- Click **Copy** on the toolbar, and then click **Paste.**
- Click **Edit | Duplicate**.

The first method places the copy in the upper-left corner of the design. The other three methods place the copy just below the original. After making as many copies as you need, you can drag them around in the design.

3. To remove a control from the form or report design, select the control, and then either:

- Press **DELETE**.

    –Or–

- Click **Edit | Delete**.

If you change your mind, click **Undo** or click **Edit | Undo**.

Rearrange Controls

Even if you used wizards to create controls for your form or report, you will probably want to make some changes. Before you can make any control changes, you will need to select the control.

SELECT CONTROLS

You have two ways to select a single control:

- Click the **Object down arrow** on the Formatting toolbar, and select the name of the control from the list.
- Click the control.

If you want to make the same changes to several controls, select them all before making the changes using one of the following methods:

- Hold down **SHIFT** while you click each control.
- **To select a column or row of controls**, click the horizontal ruler above the controls or the vertical ruler left of the controls.
- **To select a block of controls**, click one of the rulers and drag to draw a rectangle in the form design around the controls. This selects all controls within or partially within the rectangle.
- **To select a block of controls that do not include a complete row or column**, click in the design outside of any control and drag a rectangle around the controls.
- **To select all the controls in the form design**, click **Edit | Select All**. You can also press **CTRL+A** to select all controls.

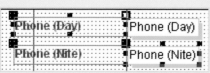

Select a column of controls

Customers Form : Form

Book Customers

Form Header

Detail

CusID — CusID — Phone (Day) — Phone (Day)
Last Name — Last Name — Phone (Nite) — Phone (Nite)
First Name — First Name — Last Order — Last Order
Company — Company — Credit Limit — Credit Limit
Address1 — Address1 — Bal Due — Bal Due

When you select a control, you will see a set of small dark squares around it. These are the *handles*. The larger squares are the *move handles*, and the smaller ones are *sizing handles*.

Once one or more controls have been selected, you can move, resize, align, adjust spacing, and change their properties, individually (if only one is selected) or as a group.

MOVE AND RESIZE CONTROLS

To move a control, rest the mouse pointer on the **move handle**, and when the mouse pointer turns into an open hand, drag the control to another location. Then drop it where you want it.

Text boxes have two move handles, so you can move the edit region and label together or separately.

- If the mouse pointer shows an **open (or grabber) hand**, they will move together.
- If the mouse pointer shows a **pointing hand**, only that element moves when you click and drag.

If you have selected a group of controls, moving one control moves all the controls together.

To resize a control, drag one of the sizing handles. Dragging a corner sizing handle can change both the height and width at once. If you have selected a group of controls, they are all resized at once.

The Format menu includes some special sizing commands you can apply to a single control or to a group of controls.

1. Select the control or group of controls, then either:

- Click **Format | Size**.

  –Or–

- Right-click and point to **Size** in the context menu.

2. Select the Size option you want from the following:

- **To Fit** resizes a single control to fit its contents.
- **To Grid** resizes a control so that all four corners reach the nearest grid points.
- **To Tallest**, **To Shortest**, **To Widest**, and **To Narrowest** all adjust the size of all other members of the group to fit one.

Size	▶	XY	To Fit
Horizontal Spacing	▶		To Grid
Vertical Spacing	▶		To Tallest
Group			To Shortest
Ungroup			To Widest
Bring to Front			To Narrowest

ALIGN AND SPACE CONTROLS

The aligning and spacing options apply to groups of controls. Forms look more professional when the elements are lined up evenly and are equally spaced.

1. Select one of the members in the group then either:

- Click **Format | Align**.

  –Or–

- Right-click and point to **Align** on the context menu.

2. Choose from the Align choices:

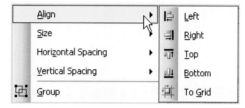

- **Left** places all controls in a column with the left sides lined up.

- **Right** places all controls in a column with the right sides lined up.

- **Top** places all controls in a row with the top sides lined up.

- **Bottom** places all controls in a row with the bottom sides lined up.

- **To Grid** places the upper left corner of all controls on a grid mark.

Forms and reports look better if the controls are evenly spaced. You can use the horizontal and vertical spacing options to space the controls uniformly or increase/decrease spacing.

Click **Format | Horizontal Spacing** or **Format | Vertical Spacing**, or use the context menu and choose one of the following options:

- **Make Equal**, to fix the controls at the left and right (horizontal) or top and bottom (vertical) and move the others to equalize the intervening spacing

- **Increase** or **Decrease**, to fix the controls at the left and top and increase or decrease the space between the others by one grid space

Modify Controls

Once controls are placed in the form design, you can still make changes in their appearance and behavior. To modify a control, select it as described in "Select Controls," earlier in this section, then change its properties, switch to a different control type, or copy its format to other controls.

CHANGE CONTROL PROPERTIES

Controls in forms and reports all have properties that set their appearance and behavior. The property sheet contains lists of all the properties that apply to the selected control, arranged by category.

To open the property sheet for a control do one of the following:

- Double-click the control.
- Select the control and click **View | Properties**.
- Select the control and click the **Properties** toolbar button.
- Right-click the control and choose **Properties** from the context menu.

The lists of properties in the sheet depend on the type of control you have selected. Figure 6-17 shows the property sheet for a text box control.

Figure 6-17: You can set numerous properties for a text box control.

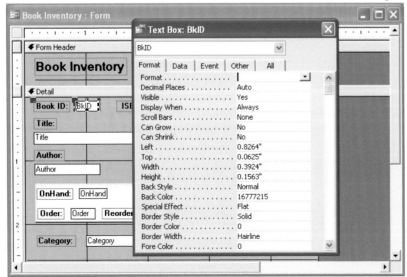

Click the tab that contains the type of property you want to set, or click the **All** tab to see them all. A scroll bar indicates there are more properties than are visible at the moment.

To change a property, click the property and then do one of the following:

- Type the setting in the property box.
- Click the **down arrow** and select the setting from the list.
- Click the **Build (...)** button to get help from a builder or from a dialog box with a choice of builders. What shows up depends on the type of control you have selected.

TIP

When you click a property, you can see a description of the property in the status bar.

NOTE

When you change a control to another type, applicable properties are copied to the new control. Properties that don't apply to the new type are ignored. Properties that weren't used in the original control but apply to the new type are assigned default settings.

If you have selected more than one control, the properties displayed in the property sheet are limited to those common to all the selected control types.

To set properties for another control, keep the property sheet open while you select the next control. When you have finished setting the properties, close the property sheet.

CHANGE TO A DIFFERENT CONTROL TYPE

If the type of control you placed in the form isn't what you want, you probably won't have to start over with a new control. You can often change the control to another type.

Not all controls can convert to any other type. Here are the rules:

- Labels can convert only to text boxes.
- Text boxes, combo boxes, and list boxes can convert from one to another.
- The Yes/No controls—check boxes, toggle buttons, and option buttons—can also convert from one to another.

Figure 6-18: The Change To menu offers to change the control type.

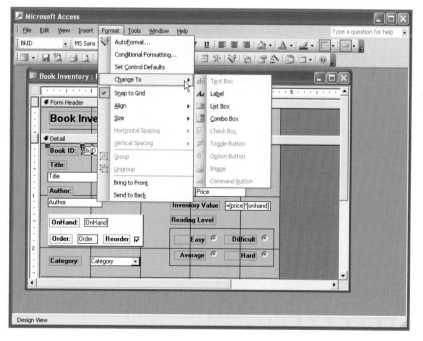

QUICKSTEPS

NAVIGATING IN A DATA ENTRY FORM

When you use a form for data entry, you usually press **TAB** to move from one field to another. The order in which you move through the fields was determined by the sequence in which you added the fields to the design. If you have rearranged them, you may not have a smooth trail through the data. To fix this:

1. Open the form in Design view.
2. Select the **Detail** section.
3. Click **View | Tab Order**.
4. Select **Detail**.
5. Either click **Auto Order** to build a path left to right, then top to bottom; or click in the field selection box (the gray square at the left of the field name), and drag it to a new position in the list. Repeat with other fields as necessary.
6. Click **OK** when the fields are in the desired order.

To change a control:

1. Select the control you want to change.
2. Click **Format | Change To**. Figure 6-18 shows a list of controls to which the current one can be converted. If the control type is dimmed in the list, it is not a candidate.
3. Click the new type of control.

COPY A CUSTOM CONTROL FORMAT

Once you have set all the format properties for a control, you can copy these settings and apply them to other controls.

1. Select the control.
2. Click **Properties** on the Form Design toolbar, and then click the **Format** tab.
3. Enter the settings.
4. Click the **Format Painter**.
5. Click the control to apply the format.
6. Repeat Steps 4 and 5 for each control you want to share the same format.

Chapter 7
Working with Reports

Access provides numerous ways to display your information in printed format (see Chapter 8 for information on printing). For the best physical display, however, using *reports* is the way to go, as shown in Figure 7-1. Within reports, you can control the size and appearance of each item, allowing you complete control over the spotlight of each page. This chapter will take you through the basics of report creation, starting with using the built-in wizards and ending with a "do-it-yourself" approach, using the Design view.

Create Reports

Reports provide a method for presenting information residing within tables and queries. This information may be presented in its current format or manipulated to display comparisons, subtotals, and totals. Although the latter can be accomplished by using queries, reports achieve this task with much less effort. The construction of reports is very similar to building forms. Because of this, you will note Chapter 6 references to detailed techniques of working with the similar tools or objects are provided.

Figure 7-1: Reports present and calculate data.

QUICKSTEPS

VIEWING REPORTS

When working with reports, it is helpful to understand how to navigate through the different views and the purpose for each view. Open a database and select **Reports** in the Database window to view all existing reports.

VIEW REPORTS IN PRINT PREVIEW

Select a report and click **Preview**, or double-click the report to open it in Print Preview mode. This will look very similar to the Print Preview windows found in other Office products, such as Word and Excel. It provides a view of the entire document as it would look in printed form. Click the image to zoom between the report's actual size (100%) and the size that best fits inside the Print Preview window.

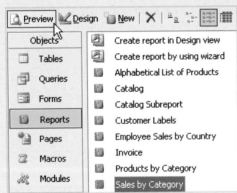

VIEW REPORTS IN DESIGN VIEW

Design view is the place to go when creating or modifying your reports. First sight of Design view bombards the eye with boxes, called controls, and dotted grid patterns, as shown in Figure 7-2. It is in this view that you are able to create or control the displayed report by changing anything from the underlying data source to the color of the text.

Continued...

Sales by Year

27-Jan-2004

2003 Summary

Quarter:	Orders Shipped:	Sales:
1	92	$143,703
2	92	$145,855
3	166	$208,305
4	191	$304,500
Totals	541	$802,163

2003 Details

Line Number:	Shipped Date:	Order ID:	Sales
1	1-Jan-2003	10392	$1,440
2	2-Jan-2003	10397	$717
3	3-Jan-2003	10393	$2,557
4	3-Jan-2003	10394	$442
5	3-Jan-2003	10395	$2,123
6	6-Jan-2003	10396	$1,904
7	8-Jan-2003	10399	$1,766
8	8-Jan-2003	10404	$1,591
9	9-Jan-2003	10398	$2,506
10	9-Jan-2003	10403	$855
11	0-Jan-2003	10401	$3,869

Page 1 of 25

VIEWING REPORTS (Continued)

Select a report and click **Design View**, or if already in Print Preview, click the **View** button once to toggle to Design view.

VIEW REPORTS IN LAYOUT VIEW

If you're working with a large report, you may want to see the layout of the report with only a sampling of records. Layout view allows you to do just that.

Open a report in Design view, as described above, and click the **View down arrow** on the Report Design toolbar. Click **Layout Preview**.

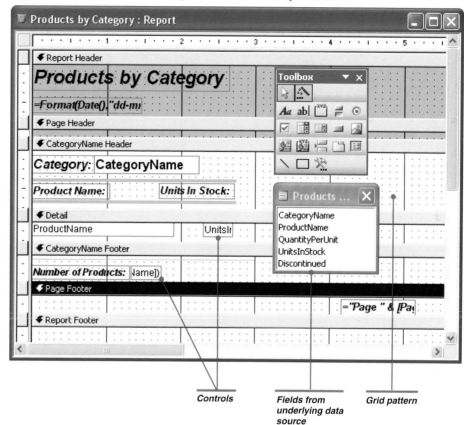

Controls   Fields from underlying data source   Grid pattern

Use AutoReport to Create a Report

The quickest way to create a report is to use AutoReport. It creates a report that displays all fields and records in the underlying table or query. Using AutoReport necessitates the report be based on a single table or query. Its structure can be either columnar or tabular.

1. In the Database window, click **Reports**.

2. Click **New** on the Database window toolbar. The New Report dialog box will be displayed.

3. In the **New Report** dialog box, click one of the following wizards:

   ● **AutoReport: Columnar**, to display each field on a separate line with a label to its left

   –Or–

   ● **AutoReport: Tabular**, to display the fields in each record on one line, and print the labels once at the top of each page

4. Select the table or query that contains the data on which you want your reports based. Click the **down arrow** next to Choose The Table Or Query Where The Object's Data Comes From, and select a table or query whose data you want to use in the report, as shown in Figure 7-3.

5. Click **OK**. Your report will be displayed in Print Preview.

TIP

AutoReport generates a report using the last style you selected using the Report Wizard or AutoFormat within the Report Design view.

Figure 7-3: AutoReport can only use data from one table or query.

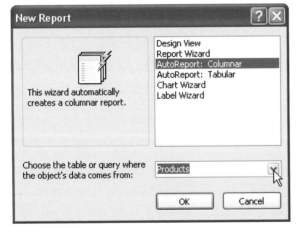

Use the Report Wizard to Create a Report

If you would like to include a few or several tables and queries in one report, the Report Wizard is your quickest way to creation.

1. In the Database window, click **Reports**.

2. Double-click **Create Report By Using Wizard** to launch the Report Wizard.

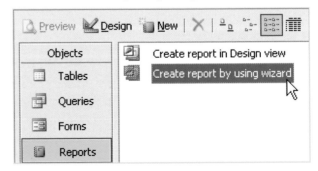

SELECT FIELDS FOR YOUR REPORT

In the first step of the Report Wizard, shown in Figure 7-4, you will select the fields you want in your report.

Figure 7-4: You can add fields from several tables and queries when using the Report Wizard.

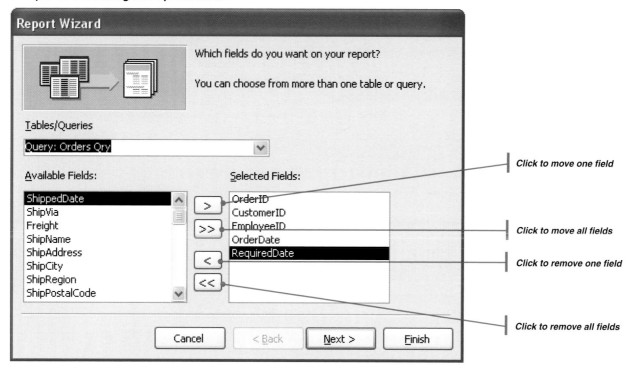

Click to move one field

Click to move all fields

Click to remove one field

Click to remove all fields

1. Click the **Tables/Query down arrow**, scroll the list, and select a table or query.

2. Click the **single right arrow** to choose individual fields from the Available Fields list, or the **double right arrow** to choose all fields. The fields will be displayed in the Selected Fields box.

3. If you are unsatisfied with the chosen results, click the **double left arrow** to remove all the fields, or the **single left arrow** to remove individual fields from the Selected Fields box.

4. Repeat Steps 1 through 3 if you want to include fields from other tables or queries. Click **Next** when finished adding fields.

VIEW THE WIZARD'S CHOICE OF GROUPING LEVELS

If you choose fields from several tables or queries, the wizard tries to establish natural groups within the data based on the relationships between tables. The second step is the wizard's effort at grouping the fields for you. Either:

● Accept the wizard's grouping, and click **Next** to move to the third step.

–Or–

● If you would rather set your own criteria for grouping levels, select another table in the How Do You Want To View Your Data list box. This will deselect the wizard's grouping choice. Click **Next** to move to the third step.

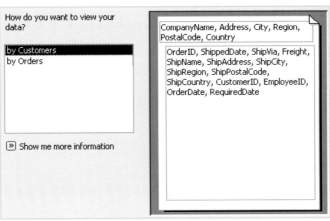

ESTABLISH YOUR OWN GROUPING LEVELS

1. Select the field you would like to group information under, and click the **right arrow** to add it to the grouping level.

2. You can adjust the priority of each group by selecting the group and clicking the **up** or **down arrow**, relative to the priority level. Continue selecting fields until you have established your grouping levels. Click **Next**.

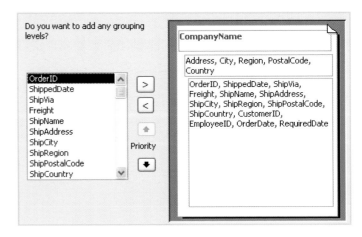

DETERMINE SORT ORDER AND SUMMARY INFORMATION

In the wizard's next step, specify any additional sort orders for the detail fields.

1. Select a field in the sort order box, as shown in Figure 7-5.

2. If you would like to change the sort method from ascending to descending, click **Ascending** and it will toggle to Descending.

3. If you would like to add additional sort fields, repeat steps 1 and 2. You can choose up to four sort fields.

Figure 7-5: Use Summary Options to create calculated group values.

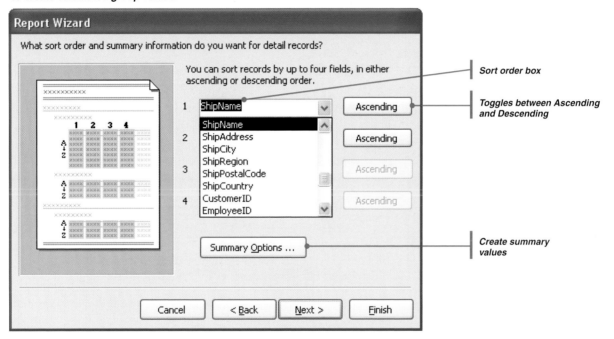

4. To create summary values in the group footers, click **Summary Options**. This opens a dialog box that makes it easy to calculate and display summary values for any grouped numeric fields the wizard finds in the Detail section. Do one or more of the following:

- Click the calculation you would like for each detail field. You can select multiple options.

- If you only want to see the totals for each group, select **Summary Only** in the Show area. If individual detail amounts are preferred, select **Detail And Summary**.

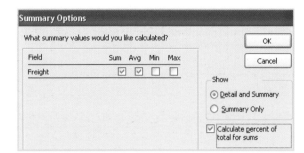

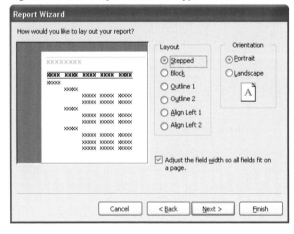

Figure 7-6: Select layout based on type of data.

- By selecting the **Calculate Percent Of Total For Sums** check box (when you have selected the Sum option), the wizard will display an additional field that shows the percent of the grand total this sum represents.

- Click **OK** in the Summary Options dialog box. Click **Next**.

ESTABLISH LAYOUT AND STYLE OF REPORT

The next two steps of the Report Wizard offer choices of layout and style. Select the layout descriptions to view the examples, as shown in Figure 7-6.

1. Choose the layout and page orientation, and determine whether to adjust the field widths so all fields fit on a page. Click **Next**.

2. Choose the style that fits your design needs and click **Next**.

CREATE THE REPORT TITLE

In the Report Wizard's last step, you specify the report title by accepting the default title or typing a new one in the text box. You also can choose to preview the report or to open it in Design view to make additional modifications. Click **Finish**.

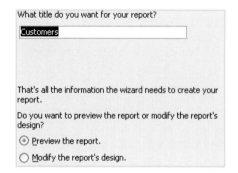

Create a Report in Design View

When creating a report in Design view, it is helpful to see the framework of a report. Figure 7-7 is an example of the view you will see when first entering Design view. There are five sections to the report, each with its own purpose, as listed in Table 7-1.

TABLE 7-1: REPORT SECTIONS

SECTION	DESCRIPTION
Report Header	Contains information printed once at the beginning of the report (report title, company logo, author)
Page Header	Contains information printed at the top of every page (page numbers, dates)
Detail	Contains records or query results
Page Footer	Contains information printed at the bottom of every page
Report Footer	Contains information printed once at the bottom of the last page

Figure 7-7: Click controls and select a space in the grid to begin designing your report.

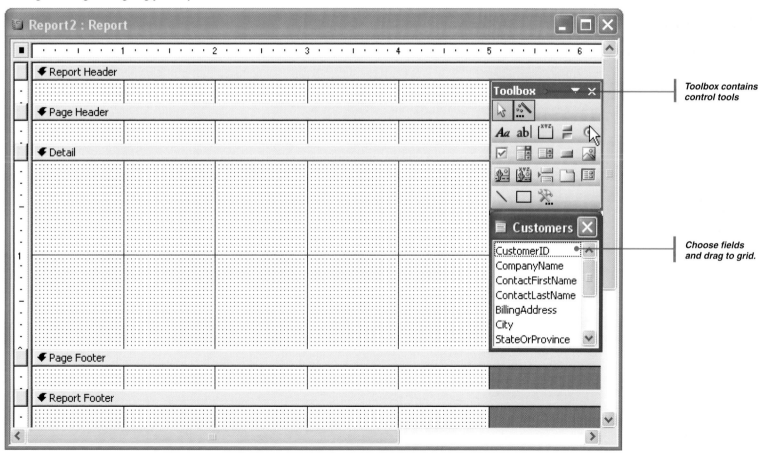

Toolbox contains control tools

Choose fields and drag to grid.

A toolbox of report controls is provided within Design view. These controls can be selected from the toolbox and placed in the grid accordingly. The controls may be *bound* (linked directly to underlying data), or *unbound* (not connected to a record source). See "Explore the Toolbox Tools," in Chapter 6, for more information about commonly used tools and their purpose. The *field list* provides the names of fields from an underlying table or query. When creating a basic report, you can simply drag fields to the grid. The tools can then be added to enhance your basic report (see "Add Bound Controls" and "Add Unbound Controls," in Chapter 6).

TIP

To create a report using data from more than one table, create a query to combine the tables and then base your report on that query. See Chapter 5 for information on creating queries.

1. In the Database window, click **Reports**.

2. Click **New** on the Database window toolbar.

3. In the New Report dialog box, click **Design View**.

4. Click the **down arrow** to open the drop-down list box, and select the table or query that contains the data you want to use in your reports, as shown in Figure 7-8. Click **OK**.

5. Drag a field name from the list to the desired location within the report's design grid. Repeat this process until satisfied with report contents.

Figure 7-8: Table or query selection provides data for bound objects.

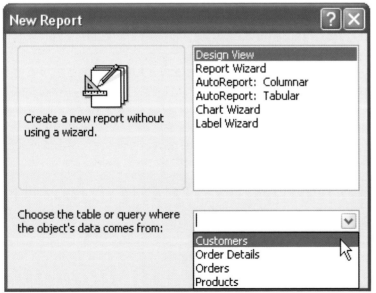

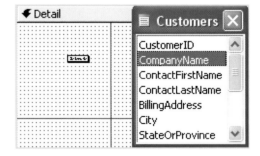

Modify Reports

Many of the modifications made to a report (or form) revolve around controls and the customization of them. To view specific information on controls and making changes within the controls, see Chapter 6. Modifications, such as grouping data, are only found in reports.

Group Data in Reports

One way reports differ from forms is in their ability to display information in groups.

1. Open a report in Design view.

2. Click **Sorting And Grouping** on the Report Design toolbar. The Sorting and Grouping dialog box will be displayed.

3. Click the first field of the Field/Expression column to display a down arrow in the right side of the field. Click the **down arrow** to display a list of fields from the underlying query or table. Select the field you would like to establish as the main group. The sort order field will automatically default to Ascending.

4. In the Group Properties area, as shown in Figure 7-9, click the **Group Header** text box to display the down arrow. Click the **down arrow** and select **Yes** to have the main group field name displayed as a group header.

5. Continue adding fields to be grouped to the Field/Expression column until you've met your grouping criteria or have entered the maximum ten grouping fields. Click **Close**.

Icon denotes main group

Click to change to Descending.

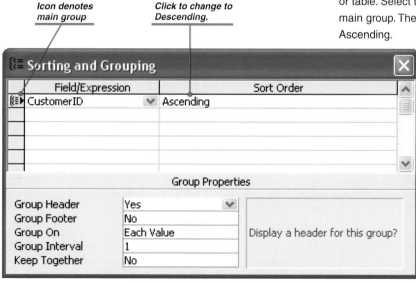

Figure 7-9: Group fields within reports to provide more visual clarity.

TIP

If the Toolbox is not visible, click the **Toolbox** on the Report Design toolbar.

Figure 7-10: The Control Source property can be an expression or a field value.

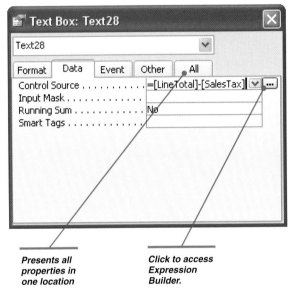

Presents all properties in one location

Click to access Expression Builder.

Calculate a Value

Reports, like queries, have the functionality to perform calculations of field values within their designs. The benefit of using a report is its ability to display the information in a customized and formatted printable fashion.

1. Open a report in Design view.

2. Click the **Text Box** tool in the toolbox. ab|

3. Click the place in the report where you would like the new calculated control.

4. Select **Properties** from the Report Design toolbar, or click **ALT+ENTER**. Click the **Data** tab, if not already selected.

5. Click inside the Control Source text box, as shown in figure 7-10, and type = followed by an expression to calculate field values. Click the three-dot **Build** button to start the Expression Builder. If you need assistance building an expression with the Expression Builder, see the QuickSteps, "Using the Expression Builder," in Chapter 5. Close the Properties dialog box.

6. In the design area, click the new text box label and click **Properties** on the Report Design toolbar.

7. Select the **All** tab and type a new label in the Caption text box.

8. Close the Properties dialog box.

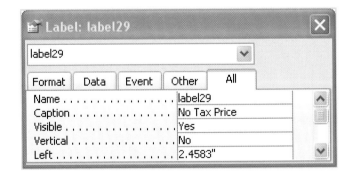

UICKSTEPS

ACCOMPLISHING COMMON TASKS IN REPORTS

Open a report in Design view.

INSERT PAGE BREAKS

1. Click the **Page Break** tool in the toolbox.

2. Click where you want the page break on the report. You will see a series of small dots at the far left side of the report. This indicates a page break in Design view.

ADD PAGE NUMBERS

1. Click **Insert | Page Numbers**. The Page Numbers dialog box is displayed.

2. Click to choose the format, position, and alignment for the page numbers, as shown in Figure 7-11. Click **OK**. A text box with the numbering information will be displayed within either the page header or page footer, based on your selection.

CREATE A REPORT TITLE

1. Click the **Label** tool in the toolbox. *Aa*

2. Click the location you want the title. (Typically, this would be in the Report Header section.)

3. Type a title in the Label box.

4. Click **Properties** on the toolbar. Select the **Format** tab, as shown in Figure 7-12, and adjust properties according to your formatting desires (see Chapter 8 for more information on formatting controls and reports).

5. Close the properties dialog box. You will see the title as it will appear on the report in either Design view or Print Preview.

Figure 7-11: Choose to show page numbers on your first page.

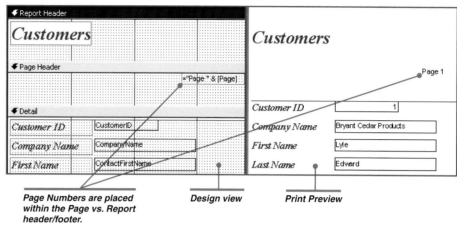

Page Numbers are placed within the Page vs. Report header/footer.

Design view

Print Preview

Figure 7-12: Format properties can be set and seen within Design view.

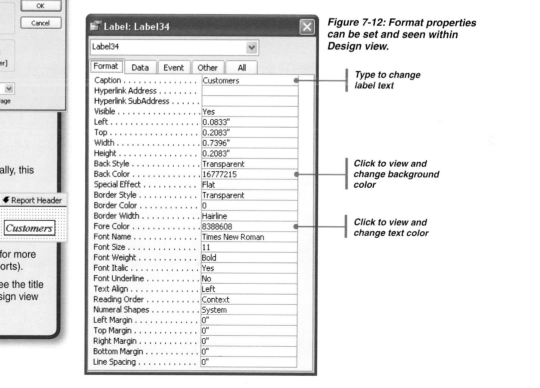

Type to change label text

Click to view and change background color

Click to view and change text color

Create a Subreport

A subreport is a report embedded in another main report. Subreports are especially useful if the tables or queries on which you are basing your main report have relationships established with other tables. See "Define Relationships," in Chapter 2 for more information about establishing relationships. If your main report is the "one" member of a one-to-many relationship, you can embed a "many" member of the relationship within the report to display multiple detail lines. For example, if you want to create a report with your customer information, but you would also like to see the orders placed by that customer, create a main report based on the customer table and a subreport based on the orders table. The tables are related as shown in Figure 7-13.

Figure 7-13: The subreport is pulled from the "many" side of a one-to-many relationship.

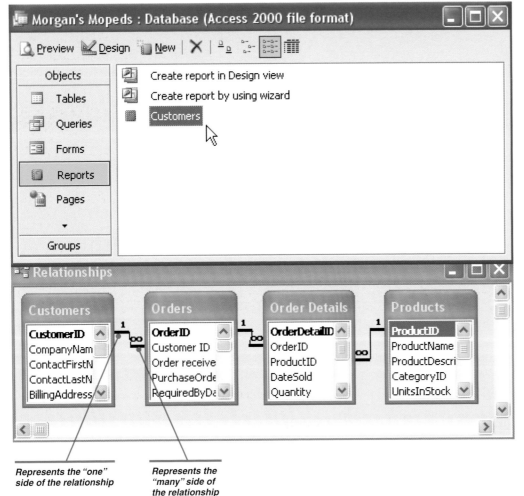

Represents the "one"
side of the relationship

Represents the
"many" side of
the relationship

1. Click the **Reports** object in the Database window, and open a report in Design view. Select a report based on a table on the "one" side of a one-to-many relationship, as shown in Figure 7-13.

3. Click the place in the report where you would like the subreport. The first dialog box of the wizard will be displayed, as shown in Figure 7-14.

4. Either:

Figure 7-14: Data can be used from tables, queries, reports, and forms.

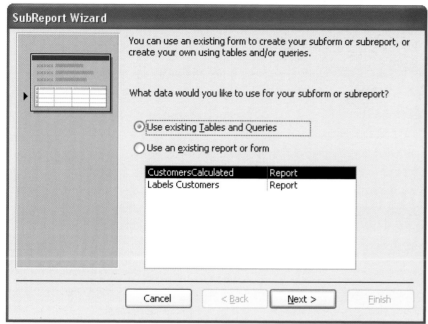

- Click **Use Existing Tables And Queries** to base the subreport on existing tables or queries. If this choice is selected, another dialog box will be displayed. Select the table or query upon which you would like to base the subreport, and move all fields to be displayed to the Selected Fields box by clicking the **right arrow**. Click **Next**.

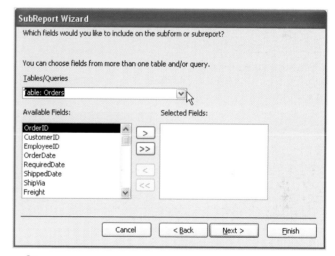

–Or–

- Click **Use An Existing Report Or Form** to base the subreport on existing reports or forms. Scroll the list of forms and reports, and select the form or report on which to base the subreport. Click **Next**.

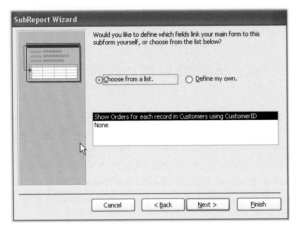

5. Select a field that will serve to link the main report to the subreport, or click to define your own linking fields. If the latter option is chosen, another dialog box will be displayed providing drop-down lists of field choices. Select the appropriate fields. Click **Next** to move to the final wizard screen.

6. Type a subreport name in the text box or accept the default name. Click **Finish**.

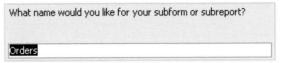

Create Labels

1. In the Database window, click **Reports**.

2. Click **New** on the Database window toolbar. The New Report dialog box will be displayed.

3. In the New Report dialog box, click **Label Wizard**.

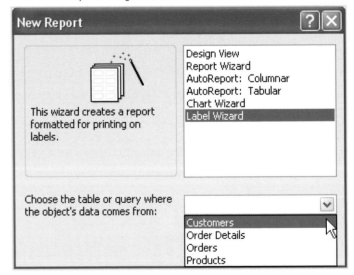

4. Select the table or query that contains the data on which you want your reports based. Click the **down arrow** next to Choose The Table Or Query Where The Object's Data Comes From and select a table or query whose data you want to use in the report. Click **OK**. The Label Wizard dialog box will be displayed.

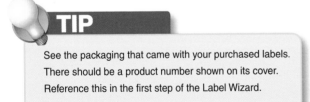

TIP

See the packaging that came with your purchased labels. There should be a product number shown on its cover. Reference this in the first step of the Label Wizard.

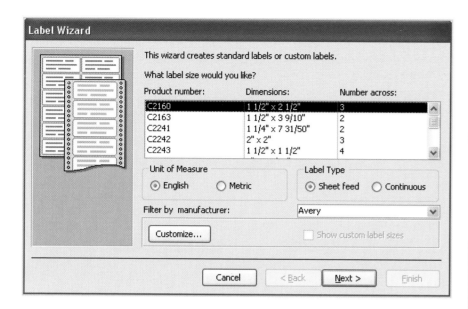

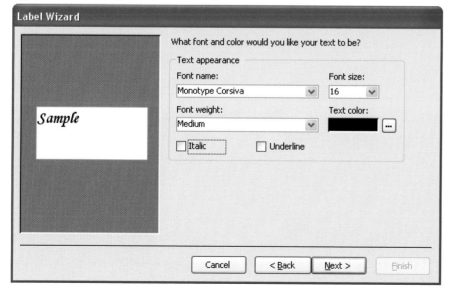

Figure 7-15: Preview your font in the sample window.

5. Select the size and type of label you would like to print. If you can't find the right size in the preset label 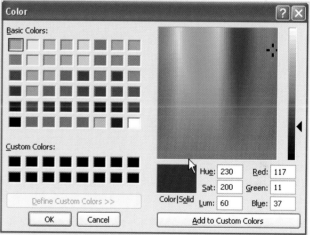 sizes, click **Customize** and set your own parameters by creating a new label definition. Click **Close** to return to the Label Wizard dialog box. Click **Next** when finished choosing or creating a label.

6. Choose the font and color you would like applied to your text, as shown in Figure 7-15. To see the available color choices, click the **Build** button to the right of the Text Color text box. Click a basic color, or click the **Define Custom Colors** button to select a custom hue. Click **OK** to return to the Label Wizard dialog box. Click **Next**.

7. Select a field you want on the label and click the **right arrow** to move it to the Prototype Label list box, as shown on the next page. If you are creating a mailing label or a label containing more than one line of text, press **ENTER** to move to the next line of the Prototype Label box. Continue selecting and moving fields until the label is designed to your liking. Click **Next**.

NOTE

To remove fields from the Prototype Label box, select the field and press **DELETE**. The deleted field remains in the Available Fields list, in case you would like to use it again.

8. Select the fields you would like to sort by and click the **right arrow** to move it to the Sort By list box. Use the direction arrows to move or remove fields from the Sort By list box. Click **Next** to move to the final screen.

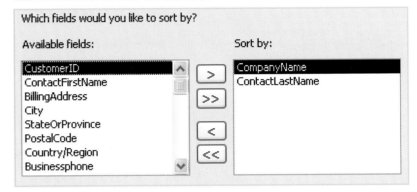

9. Type a report name in the text box or accept the default name. Click **Finish**.

NOTE

If you need to remove fields from the Prototype Label list box, select the field by dragging across it and pressing **DELETE**.

Create a Report Snapshot

You may want to distribute your report electronically to individuals who aren't using Microsoft Access. If you send the standard database file, they will be unable to use or view the information. To remedy this situation, Access provides the ability to save your report as a Report Snapshot. You can then send this snapshot, along with a Report Snapshot viewer, to anyone and allow your reports to be viewed as intended.

1. In the Database window, click **Reports**.

2. Click the report from which you want to create a report snapshot.

3. Click **File | Export**.

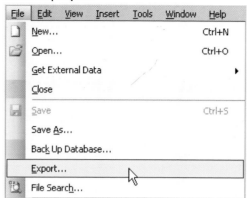

If Snapshot Viewer was not installed during your Access setup, Access will automatically install the Snapshot Viewer for you when you first try to open the snapshot.

4. Click the **Save As Type down arrow**, scroll, and select **Snapshot Format**.

5. Click the **Save In down arrow**, and select the drive or folder to export to.

Figure 7-16: Snapshot Viewer is a free, downloadable application.

6. Type the file name in the File Name box.

7. If you would like to display the results in the SnapShot Viewer, select the **AutoStart** check box. Click **Export**. ☑ Autostart
Your report will be displayed in the SnapShot Viewer, as shown in Figure 7-16.

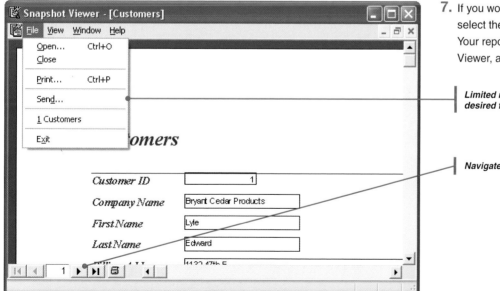

Limited menu options provide desired functionality.

Navigate through the report

Distribute a Report Snapshot

There are three methods for sending a Report Snapshot via e-mail. You can send the file directly from Snapshot Viewer or from Access, or you can send the file as an object embedded in an ActiveX-compliant electronic mail system. If you choose to use the first two methods, read below for detailed instructions. If sending directly from your e-mail client, create an e-mail as you normally would and attach the Snapshot Viewer file.

SEND DIRECTLY FROM SNAPSHOT VIEWER

1. Use Windows Explorer to find the location where the exported file is saved. (See "Create a Report Snapshot" for instructions on exporting a report to the snapshot file format.)

2. Double-click the file to open it within Snapshot Viewer.

3. Click **File| Send**, as shown in Figure 7-16. Your default mail client will open a new e-mail message and add the snapshot as an attachment. (Your e-mail program must support ActiveX controls, such as Microsoft Outlook.)

SEND FROM ACCESS

In order to use this method, your e-mail program, such as Microsoft Outlook, must support ActiveX controls.

1. Select **Reports** within the Database window. Click the report you would like to send.

2. Click **File | Send To | Mail Recipient (as Attachment)...** The Send dialog box will be displayed.

3. Click **Snapshot Format** in the Select Format list box. Click **OK**. Your default mail client will open a new e-mail message and add the snapshot as an attachment.

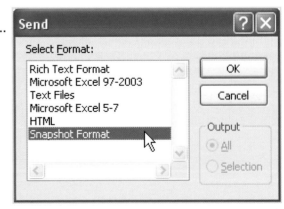

Chapter 8

Preparing Your Data for Presentation

You can make several visual enhancements to your forms and reports before you release them to be used (in the case of forms) or printed (in the case, typically, of reports). The first part of this chapter describes many of these features in addition to how you can format forms and reports in Design view. The latter part of the chapter describes further options you have when printing your data.

Improve the Data's Appearance

The judicious use of color, graphics, and lines can transform a drab collection of data into an appealing presentation for people who enter or analyze your data. The features and techniques described in this section apply to both Form and Report Design view, unless otherwise noted.

Modify Images

Chapter 6 describes how to insert images into Design view, directly or by use of the Image toolbox control (see "Insert Special Controls" in Chapter 6). This section describes changes you can make to the image after it has been placed in a Design view form or report.

CHOOSE AN IMAGE FORMAT

You can use images from several different graphics formats, as listed in Table 8-1.

FILE TYPE	EXTENSION
AutoCAD	.dxf
Bitmaps	.bmp, dib
Computer Graphics Metafile	.cgm
CorelDraw	.cdr
Encapsulated PostScript	.eps
FPX	.fpx
Graphics Interchange Format	.gif
Icons	.ico
Joint Photographic Experts Graphics	.jpg
Macintosh PICT	.pct
Metafiles	.wmf, .emf
Picture It!	.mix
Portable Network Graphics	.png
Tag Image File Format	.tif
WordPerfect Graphics	.wpg

TABLE 8-1: GRAPHICS FILES SUPPORTED BY ACCESS

NOTE

The pictures (or *images*) and graphics that are described in this chapter are *unbound* objects, meaning they are stored in the design of the form or report and do not change when you move from record to record or from page to page. *Bound* pictures, such as photos that identify each item in your antique collection, are bound to the underlying data.

CAUTION

Not all image formats are supported by Access out of the box. Many are only available when using filters supplied by Access as part of the Microsoft Professional Edition 2003 or when Microsoft Word is installed in addition to a standalone version of Access.

CHANGE IMAGE PROPERTIES

There are 19 properties specifically associated with images, as shown in Figure 8-1, that you can use to change the characteristics of images you add to a form or report. To change a property's setting, do one of the following:

● **Type a value**. For example, to precisely change the location of an image in the form or report section it's in, type units of measurement in the Left and Top property text boxes. The intersection of these two numbers defines the location of the upper-left corner of the image.

Left	3.3285"
Top	3.3285"
Width	1.5"
Height	0.7653"

- **Click the property's down arrow**, and select a setting from the drop-down list. For example, to decrease the size of your database, you could change each image file Picture Type from being *embedded* (each file becomes part of the .mdb file) to *linked* (a pointer is placed in the database to the actual location of the image file outside the database). See Chapter 10 for more information on linking.

Picture Type	Embedded
Size Mode	Embedded
Picture Alignment	Linked

- **Click the Build button** to open a dialog box for supplementary information. For example, clicking the Picture property Build button opens the Insert Picture dialog box, where you can change the location of the present image, or browse to a new image.

Format	Data	Event	Other	All
Picture			C:\Documents and Settir	...
Picture Type			Embedded	
Size Mode			Clip	

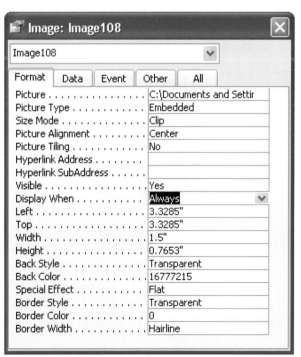

Figure 8-1: You have a great many formatting properties available to you when working with images.

Add a Chart

You can add *charts* by importing them from other programs, such as Microsoft Excel; by creating your own using the menus and tools of Excel within Access; or by using the Access Chart Wizard.

IMPORT AN EXCEL CHART

1. In Excel, ensure that the chart is on the *active* worksheet or chartsheet.

2. Open the report or form in Design view, and select the section where you want the chart placed (see "Select Design View Components," later in the chapter).

3. Click **Insert | Object** and select **Create From File**, shown in Figure 8-2.

4. Click **Browse** and locate the Excel workbook (.xls) that contains the chart. Double-click the file in the Browse dialog box.

5. Choose how you want the worksheet or chartsheet containing the chart to be attached to Access. Do either, neither, or both:

   - Select the **Link** check box to create a connection between the workbook file and the object in the report or form. Changes to the source worksheet or chartsheet will be reflected in Access.

   - Select the **Display As Icon** check box to add the worksheet or chartsheet as an icon that will open the full object when double-clicked. You can create icons for both linked and embedded objects.

6. Click **OK**. If you didn't choose to link the worksheet or chartsheet, it will be added as an embedded object.

Figure 8-2: You can insert existing objects from other programs as embedded or linked files.

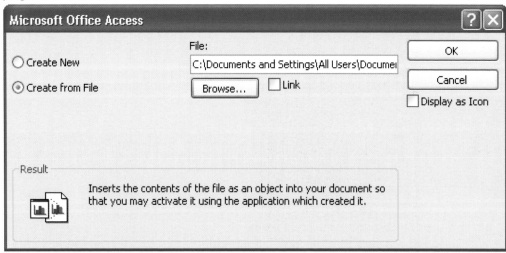

CREATE A CHART USING EXCEL FEATURES

1. Open the report or form in Design view, and select the section where you want the chart placed.

2. Click **Insert | Object** and select **Create New**.

3. In the Object Type list box, choose **Microsoft Excel Chart** and click **OK**. A sample chart opens in Design view, and many of the Access menus and toolbars are replaced by those of Microsoft Excel, as shown in Figure 8-3.

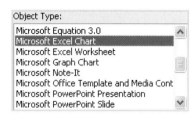

4. Click **Chart Wizard** on the Excel Formatting toolbar, or use the Chart menu and toolbars to build the chart.

5. Click outside the chart to return to full Access functionality. To edit the chart with Excel features, double-click it.

Figure 8-3: You can create an Excel chart within Access.

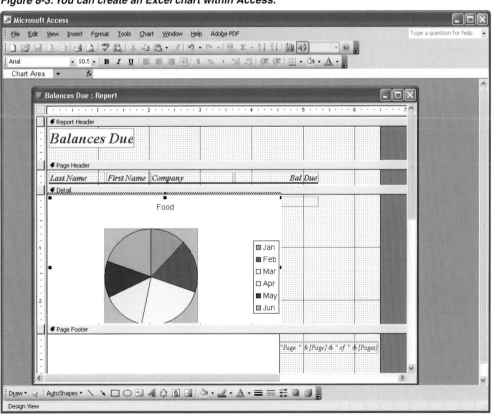

CREATE A CHART USING ACCESS

1. Open the report or form in Design view, and click the section where you want the chart placed.

2. Click **Insert | Chart** and drag a rectangle to the size and location you want the chart in the section. Perform the following actions in the Chart Wizard that is displayed, clicking **Next** between steps:

3. Determine the table or query whose data you want to use.

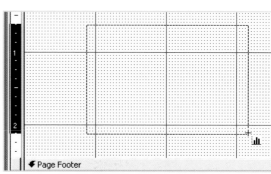

4. Select the fields from the table or query that contain the data you want to see charted.

5. Choose a chart type. Click a chart type to see its description displayed in the wizard, as shown in Figure 8-4.

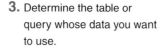

6. Drag field boxes onto the sample chart. Click **Preview Chart** to see how you're doing.

7. To have the chart reflect changes record-by-record, link the fields in the form or report to the field on the chart.

8. Type a title for the chart, and choose whether to display a legend for the data series.

9. Click **Finish**.

Figure 8-4: You have almost too many chart types to choose from!

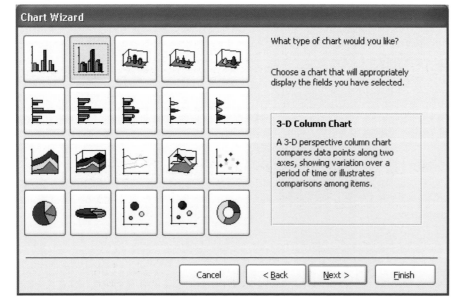

Use Graphics

Though Access doesn't provide the full breadth of drawing tools available in other Office programs, you can still be quite creative by using lines and rectangles to separate, encompass, or emphasize areas in your forms and reports.

ADD LINES AND RECTANGLES

1. Open the report or form in Design view, and click the section where you want the line or rectangle placed.

2. Click **Toolbox** on the Report/Form Design toolbar to display the toolbox if it is not already open.

3. Click the **Line** or **Rectangle** tool in the toolbar, and drag in the Design view section to the approximate size, location, and orientation you want. To more precisely arrange the graphic where you want it, either:

- Drag the sizing handles and grabber hand to resize and relocate.

- Use the applicable property to set width, height, and location (see the next section, "Modify Graphics Properties").

USING THE FORMATTING TOOLBAR

The Formatting toolbar offers shortcuts to tools that specify the appearance of the controls, graphics, and the objects themselves in Design view. The tools that are available to you, shown in Figure 8-5, will depend on the item selected. To display the Formatting toolbar, do either:

- Click **View | Toolbars | Formatting (Form/Report)**.
- Right-click the menu bar/toolbar area, and select **Formatting (Form/Report)**.

Figure 8-5: The Formatting toolbar in Design view provides quick access to formatting features.

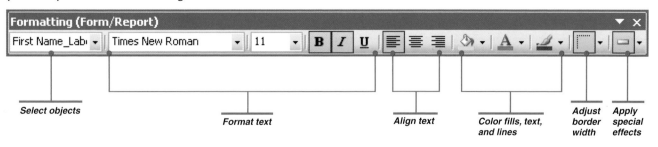

Select objects

Format text

Align text

Color fills, text, and lines

Adjust border width

Apply special effects

MODIFY GRAPHICS PROPERTIES

1. Click the graphic to select it, and click **Properties** on the Report/Form Design toolbar or right-click the graphic and select **Properties**.

2. Change the settings for the property you want (see "Change Image Properties," earlier in the chapter, for ways to change property settings).

Modify the Form or Report Design

Forms and reports have several properties that determine their appearance and behavior.

SELECT DESIGN VIEW COMPONENTS

Before you can work on a particular section of a form or report, you need to select it. Do one or more of the following:

● To select the object itself, click **Edit | Select Form** (or **Edit | Select Report**), click the object selector (box at the intersection of the rulers), or click anywhere in the background outside the form/report design.

● To select a form or report section, click the form/report section selector—the small square in the vertical ruler next to the section divider (If the ruler and/or grid is not displayed, click **View | Ruler** or **View | Grid** to turn them on.)

● To select controls, click a single control, press and hold SHIFT while clicking multiple controls, or drag a selection rectangle around the controls you want in the selection.

● To select all items on the report or form, click **Edit | Select All** or press CTRL+A.

TIP

You can select specific controls in Design view by clicking the **Object down arrow** on the Formatting toolbar and selecting the control by name.

TIP

If the window containing a form in Form view is not maximized and shows a lot of blank space around it, you can resize the window to fit the form by clicking **Window | Size to Fit Form**; then click **Save** on the Form View toolbar to keep the new dimensions.

Figure 8-6: You have ample opportunity to customize a report through its properties.

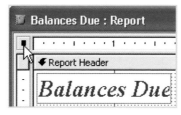

NOTE

See Chapter 6 for information on aligning and spacing controls in Design view.

CHANGE FORM AND REPORT PROPERTIES

1. Open the form or report in Design view.

2. Click the form/report selector at the intersection of the horizontal and vertical rulers.

3. Click **Properties** on the Report/Form Design toolbar.

4. Click the **Format** tab. Figure 8-6 shows a partial list of the format properties you can set for a report. Other tabs in the property sheet offer data, event, and other properties.

5. Click the **down arrow** next to a property to see a list of choices.

6. Type a value, select from the list of settings, or click the **Build** button.

7. When finished, close the property sheet and click **View** on the Report or Form Design toolbar to see your changes.

FORMAT AUTOMATICALLY

When you created a form or report with its respective wizard, you had a choice of layout and style. You can modify these designs manually, as described earlier in this chapter, and you can select from pre-built formats.

1. Open the form or report in Design view, and click **AutoFormat** on the Form or Report Design toolbar or click **Format | AutoFormat**.

2. In the AutoFormat dialog box, shown in Figure 8-7, select the style you want.

3. Click **Options** to open the Attributes to Apply pane, and select the elements you want affected by the new style.

4. Click **OK**.

Figure 8-7: Change a form and report style with AutoFormat.

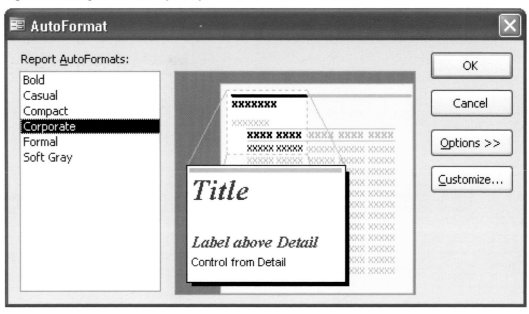

NOTE

If you want to create and save your own customized AutoFormat, click **Customize** in the AutoFormat dialog box.

Print Your Data

Access provides a broad array of printing options, many tailored to the object you are interested in printing.

Set Up the Print Job

You can modify several printing features in the Page Setup dialog box that affect the printed page, and you can review the page prior to print in Print Preview. Some features are not available for all objects you want to print (for example, datasheets and queries don't let you change columnar settings) and only affect printing of the current object (though the settings are retained for the next time you print the same object).

Changing margin settings in the Page Setup dialog box affects printing of the current object only. To change margin settings for all objects, click **Tools | Options** and select the **General** tab. Type new margin settings in the Print Margins area.

```
┌─ Print margins ──────────────────────────────┐
│                                              │
│   Left margin:        [ 1.5"        ]        │
│                                              │
│   Right margin:       [ 1.5"        ]        │
│                                              │
│   Top margin:         [ 1"          ]        │
│                                              │
│   Bottom margin:      [ 1"          ]        │
└──────────────────────────────────────────────┘
```

ADJUST MARGINS

You can adjust the distance between edges of the printed page and where text and pictures are printed for the current object.

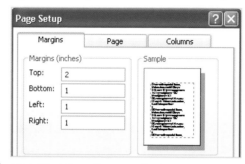

1. Click **File | Page Setup** and select the **Margins** tab.

2. Adjust the Top, Bottom, Left, and Right text boxes to the respective margin you want by typing new values. As you make changes, the preview area shows the new location of the margin you are working on.

3. Click **OK** when finished making all changes in the Page Setup dialog box.

CHANGE PAPER LAYOUT, SIZE, AND SOURCE

1. Click **File | Page Setup** and select the **Page** tab. Do one or both of the following:

   • In the Orientation area, select the layout—**Portrait** (tall) or **Landscape** (wide)—that works best for how your data is arranged.

   • In the Paper area, click the **Size down arrow** and select the paper size you want. Click the **Source down arrow** and choose a specific paper location for your printer to match the size you chose.

2. Click **OK** when finished making all changes in the Page Setup dialog box.

CHOOSE A PRINTER

You can use a printer other than the default printer to print the current object, and it will be "remembered" whenever you want to print the object again. You can always choose a printer when you print from the Print dialog box (see the QuickSteps, "Choosing What To Print," later in the chapter), but it will revert to the default printer the next time you print.

1. Click **File | Page Setup** and select the **Page** tab.

2. Select **User Specific Printer** and click **Printer**. The Printer area from the Print dialog box is displayed in an abbreviated Page Setup dialog box, shown in Figure 8-8.

> Printer...

Figure 8-8: You can choose a printer that will be "remembered" each time you print the same object.

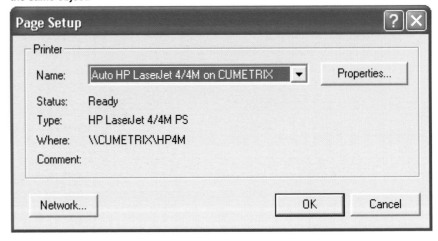

3. Click the **Name down arrow** and select a printer (if necessary, click **Network** to locate printers connected to your network that don't appear in the Name drop-down list). Click **OK** to close the abbreviated Page Setup dialog box.

4. Click **OK** when finished making all changes in the Page Setup dialog box.

Figure 8-9: You can choose whether to print forms and reports in single or multiple columns.

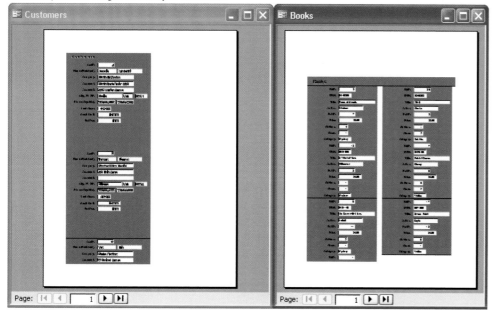

CHANGE COLUMNAR PRINT SETTINGS

The output from a report, or the labels and fields in Form view, are printed together as a column. You can make more efficient use of paper by aligning the printed data into more than one column, as shown in Figure 8-9.

1. Open a form or report. Click **File | Page Setup** and select the **Columns** tab.

2. Do one or more of the following:

- In the Grid Setting area, type how many columns you want (your paper width and column width will be determining factors) and determine the sizing between rows and columns.

- In the Column Size area, select the **Same As Detail** check box to print the column the same size as you set up in the form or report Design view. To adjust the column width and row height, deselect the check box and type new values.

- In the Column Layout area (multiple columns only), choose the direction you want the columns printed.

3. Click **OK** when finished making all changes in the Page Setup dialog box.

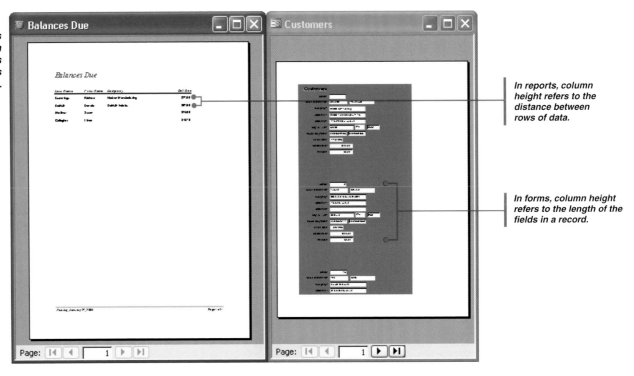

Figure 8-10: Settings for printed column heights for forms yield different results from those in reports.

In reports, column height refers to the distance between rows of data.

In forms, column height refers to the length of the fields in a record.

Page: |◄ ◄ 1 ► ►|

Page: |◄ ◄ 1 ► ►|

Review Data Before Printing

Print Preview provides a very accurate picture of your data and layout so that you can make changes before committing to expending ink/toner and paper.

OPEN THE OBJECT IN PRINT PREVIEW

Do one of the following:

NOTE

The Height text box in the Columns tab of the Page Setup dialog box works differently for forms and reports (see Figure 8-10). When setting the column height in reports, you are determining the height of each line, or row, of data printed. In forms, the Height value determines the cumulative length of all fields for each record displayed in the form.

- For **tables**, select the table in the Database window or open the table in Datasheet view. Click **Print Preview** on the toolbar.

- For **forms**, select the form in the Database window or open the form in Form view. Click **Print Preview** on the toolbar.

- For **reports**, select the report in the Database window; then click **Preview** on the Database window toolbar or double-click the report.

USE PRINT PREVIEW

The Print Preview window, shown in Figure 8-11, only allows you to toggle by clicking your mouse between two magnifications (100 percent and what will fit on a single page), and navigate through the pages to be printed using a navigation bar. Print Preview's other features are available from the Print Preview toolbar.

Do one or more of the following (from left to right on the Print Preview toolbar):

- Click the **View down arrow** to change the object to another view.
- Click **Print** to print to the printer specified in the Page Setup dialog box.
- Click **Zoom** to toggle magnification between 100 percent and what fits on a page.
- Click **One Page**, **Two Page**, or **Multiple Pages** to see pages in those respective configurations.
- Click the **Zoom down arrow** to select the level of magnification you want, or type the level you want and press **ENTER**.

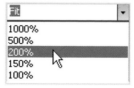

- Click **Close** to close Print Preview.
- Click **Setup** to open the Page Setup dialog box.
- Click **OfficeLinks** to export the printed pages into Word or Excel (see Chapter 10 for more information on exporting data from Access).

- Click **Database Window** to open it.
- Click the **New Object down arrow** to select the object you want to create.
- Click **Microsoft Office Access Help** to open the Access Help task pane.

Figure 8-11: Print Preview acts as a hub for your printing needs.

Print Preview toolbar

Click your mouse to toggle between magnifications.

Move through the printed pages similarly to moving through records.

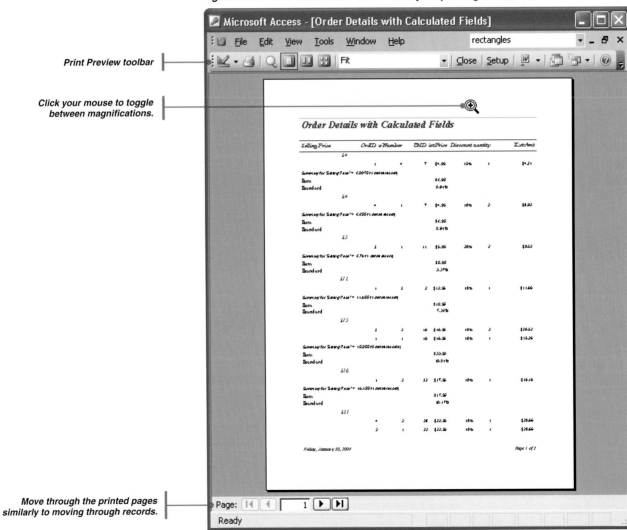

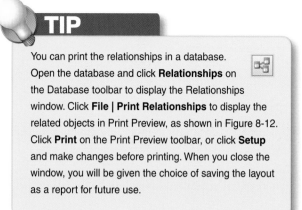

Figure 8-12: Printing a copy of the Relationships window is a great way to keep a visual representation of your database at hand.

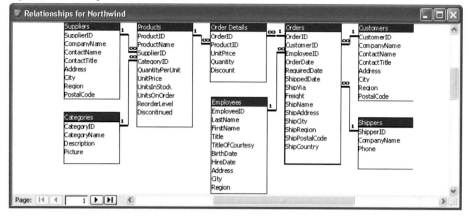

Figure 8-13: The Print dialog box provides options that control the physical aspects of printing.

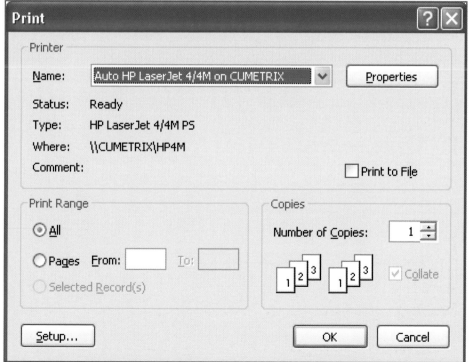

Output the Print Job

You can print to printers attached to your computer or printers on your network. You can also print to a file instead of a printer and choose features provided by your printer manufacturer. All this is accomplished from the Print dialog box, as shown in Figure 8-13, and viewed by clicking **File | Print** or by pressing **CTRL+P**.

CHOOSING WHAT TO PRINT

You have several options when you decide what portion of a database object you want printed. Depending on the object, you can print the entire table, selected pages, and selected records. Most printing options are available in the Print dialog box, shown in Figure 8-13. To open the Print dialog box, either:

- Click **File | Print**.

  –Or–

- Press **CTRL+P**.

After choosing what to print, click **OK**.

PRINT ALL PAGES

- Open the object (or run the object, in case of queries) you want to print. In the Print dialog box, under Print Range, click **All**, or click **Print** on the respective toolbar.

- Open the Database window, choose the object category, and select the object you want to print.

- Click **Print** on the Database toolbar (see the associated Note on the previous page).

PRINT SPECIFIC PAGES

In the Print dialog box, under Print Range, click **Pages**, and do one of the following:

- To print a range of pages, use the **From** and **To** spinners to set starting and ending pages.

- To print one page, set both the **From** and **To** spinners to the same page number.

- To print from a page to the last page, set only the **From** spinner.

Continued...

CHOOSE A PRINTER

In the Printer area, click the **Name down arrow** and select a printer that is installed on your computer from the drop-down list. The printer name is displayed in the Name drop-down list box, and information about the printer is listed below.

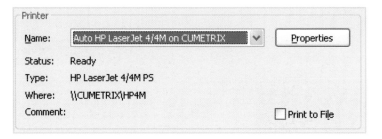

PRINT TO A FILE

You can print your printer information to a file instead of directly to a physical device. Print files are typically used to create Adobe PDF documents (you must select a Postscript printer in the Name box) or when you want to create a file of the print job to send to another computer.

1. Select **Print To File** and **OK**.

2. In the Print To File dialog box, type the path and file name of where you want the print file located, and click **OK**.

CHOOSING WHAT TO PRINT (Continued)

PRINT SPECIFIC RECORDS

1. Select the records in Datasheet view that you want to print.
2. In the Print dialog box, under Print Range, select **Selected Record(s)**.

OMIT PRINTING COLUMN HEADINGS IN DATASHEETS

1. Open the datasheet you want to print.
2. Click **File | Page Setup** and select the **Margins** tab. Deselect the **Print Headings** check box.

PRINT DATA ONLY IN FORMS AND REPORTS

You can omit printing the visual enhancements in a form or report and just print the data.

1. Open the form or report you want to print.
2. Click **File | Page Setup** and select the **Margins** tab. Select the **Print Data Only** check box.

NOTE

Newer versions of Adobe Acrobat make creating basic PDF files as easy as choosing Adobe PDF in the Printer drop-down list. If you want more control in the process, you should use the Print To File option to create a Postscript file and set up your Acrobat Distiller options to meet your specific PDF creation needs.

SELECT PRINTER-SPECIFIC OPTIONS

Most printers have additional printing options and features besides those provided in Access.

To display a printer's properties dialog box, as shown in Figure 8-14, click **Properties**.

Figure 8-14: Printers may have additional printing features besides those provided in Access.

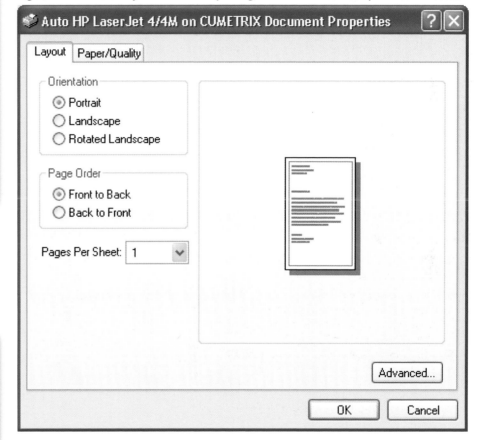

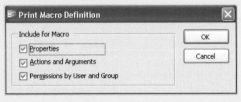
PRINT MULTIPLE COPIES

1. In the Copies area, adjust the **Number Of Copies** spinner to the number of copies you want.

2. Either:

   ● Select **Collate** to print each copy from start to finish before starting to print the next copy.

   –Or–

   ● Deselect **Collate** to print each page the number of times set in the Number Of Copies spinner before printing the next page.

Chapter 9
Securing and Administrating Access

This chapter addresses the issue of database privacy, integrity, and security. The main purpose for database security is to prevent both inadvertent and intentional damage to the data and the database objects. Proper security measures prevent anyone who might view or edit the information from gaining unauthorized access. They also prevent anyone from making design changes without express permission to do so. You can protect both the data and the design elements with a variety of approaches.

Establish User-Level Security

In a multi-user environment, security becomes both more essential and more complicated. Not all users need to have access to all the data or all the design elements in the database. One way to create security is to organize users in groups, each of which has specific responsibilities. This information is stored in the Workgroup Information file (WIF).

9

DECIDING WHO NEEDS WHAT PERMISSIONS

Depending on what the user needs to do with the database, you can assign her to any of the groups provided by the User-Level Security Wizard. To give a user more permissions than one group has, you can assign that user to more than one group.

- *Backup Operators* can open the database exclusively for backup and compacting but are not permitted to see any of the database objects.
- *Full Data Users* have full permission to edit data but are not allowed to make any design changes.
- *Full Permissions* have full permissions on all database objects but are not allowed to assign permissions to others.
- *New Data Users* can read and insert data but are not allowed to delete or update existing data. They are also not allowed to alter any object designs.
- *Project Designers* have full permission to edit data and all objects but are not allowed to alter any tables or relationships.
- *Read-Only Users* can read all the data but are not allowed to change data or any design object.
- *Update Data Users* can read and update all data but are not allowed to insert or delete data. They are also not allowed to make any design changes.

Understand the User-Level Security Model

The user-level security model is based on the idea of workgroups whose members share the data and privileges. The group and user accounts list the members of the workgroup. A *group account* is a collection of user accounts. Each member of the group is permitted some degree of freedom in dealing with data and objects. A *user account* belongs to a single user and includes the user name and personal ID (PID).

The four pieces of a user-level security model are:

- A **user** is a person who uses the database.
- A **group** is a set of users, all of whom operate at the same security level and need access to the same parts of the database.
- A **permission** gives a user or group the right to carry out a specific action. For example, Read Data permission allows opening a table or query for viewing but not for entering new data or editing existing data.
- An **object** refers to any of the Access tables, queries, forms, reports, macros, or modules —as well as to the database itself.

Secure the Database with the User-Level Security Wizard

The User-Level Security Wizard can secure any or all of the objects in your database. All the relationships and linked tables are kept intact when you secure the database with the Security Wizard. It also makes a backup copy of the original database in case you have forgotten to do so. The backup file has the same name with the *.bak* file extension.

With the Security Wizard, you can be specific about which users enjoy which permissions. You can also decide who belongs to which groups and edit user passwords and personal IDs (PIDs) as well. A PID is similar to a password and is used in combination with the user name to identify an account.

Figure 9-1: You can choose to create a new workgroup information file or edit an existing one, if available.

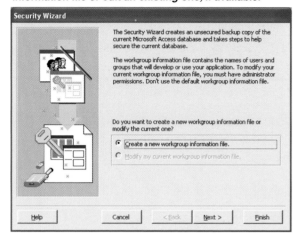

Figure 9-2: The Security Wizard lets you choose where to locate and what to name your Workgroup ID.

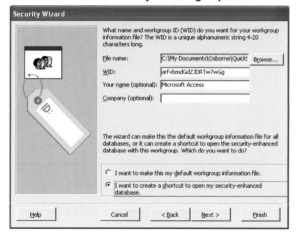

START THE USER-LEVEL SECURITY WIZARD

The database must be open before you can work with the User-Level Security Wizard.

1. Open the database whose objects you want to secure.

2. Click **Tools | Security | User-Level Security Wizard**.

3. In the first dialog box, as shown in Figure 9-1, either:

   ● Select **Create A New Workgroup Information File** if one doesn't exist.

   –Or–

   ● Select **Modify My Current Workgroup Information File** to make changes in an existing WIF.

4. Click **Next**.

5. In the next dialog box, as shown in Figure 9-2, accept the workgroup ID (WID) the Security Wizard offers or enter a unique string in the WID box. The WID is a case-sensitive string of between 4 and 20 alphabetic and numeric characters.

6. Select **I Want To Create A Shortcut To Open My Security-Enhanced Database**.

7. Click **Next**.

CAUTION

If you choose to make the WIF identified in Figure 9-2 the default, every Access database you open will use it unless you specify that it be opened with a different WIF.

TIP

Prior to using the Security Wizard, be sure to open the database in shared mode. If you open it in Exclusive mode, the Security Wizard will offer to reopen it in shared mode. Also, be sure to close any unsaved objects you have open.

NOTE

The Other tab in the third dialog box of the Security Wizard contains a list of new objects. You can choose to keep or to remove all new tables/queries, forms, reports, and macros from the Security Wizard's security program.

SECURE INDIVIDUAL OBJECTS

The third Security Wizard dialog box, shown in Figure 9-3, shows tabs for each of the objects in the current database. By default, all objects are secured by the wizard, but you can exclude some and keep the existing security measures in the others.

Figure 9-3: You can remove security from objects that don't need it.

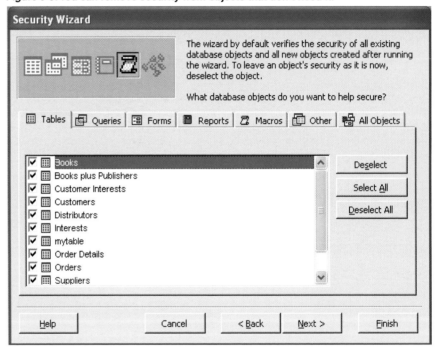

1. Deselect the check box next to the object you want to leave as it is now.
2. Click the tab (such as Queries, Forms, or Reports) for any other object whose security selections you want to change.
3. When finished, click **Next**.
4. If you have secured your Visual Basic code with a password, the Security Wizard asks for the password in the next dialog box. If not, you move on to setting up group accounts.

SET UP GROUP ACCOUNTS

Setting up group accounts involves choosing the appropriate groups for your application based on the tasks assigned to the users. In the next dialog box, shown in Figure 9-4, you can view which permissions are assigned to specific security groups, and then decide how to assign the users to the different groups. A unique group ID is assigned to each group by the Security Wizard.

Figure 9-4: The security group accounts provide specific permissions to their members.

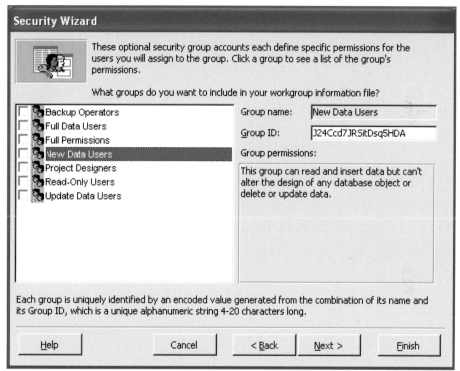

Security Wizard

These optional security group accounts each define specific permissions for the users you will assign to the group. Click a group to see a list of the group's permissions.

What groups do you want to include in your workgroup information file?

- ☐ Backup Operators
- ☐ Full Data Users
- ☐ Full Permissions
- ☐ New Data Users
- ☐ Project Designers
- ☐ Read-Only Users
- ☐ Update Data Users

Group name: New Data Users

Group ID: J24Ccd7JRSitDsq5HDA

Group permissions:

This group can read and insert data but can't alter the design of any database object or delete or update data.

Each group is uniquely identified by an encoded value generated from the combination of its name and its Group ID, which is a unique alphanumeric string 4-20 characters long.

| Help | Cancel | < Back | Next > | Finish |

CAUTION

The default Users group provides access to all objects in a database. Everyone who has a copy of Access is automatically a member of the Users group and will have the same permissions applying to all open databases.

1. Select a group in the group list to read the description of the permissions in the Group Permissions area. For example, Figure 9-4 shows the permissions granted to the New Data Users group.

2. Select the check boxes for the groups you want to include in the security model.

3. Click **Next**.

4. The next Security Wizard dialog box, shown in Figure 9-5, allows you to assign some permissions to the Users group but strongly recommends against that. Choose **No, The Users Group Should Not Have Any Permissions**.

5. Click **Next**.

Figure 9-5: The Security Wizard recommends not giving the Users group any permissions.

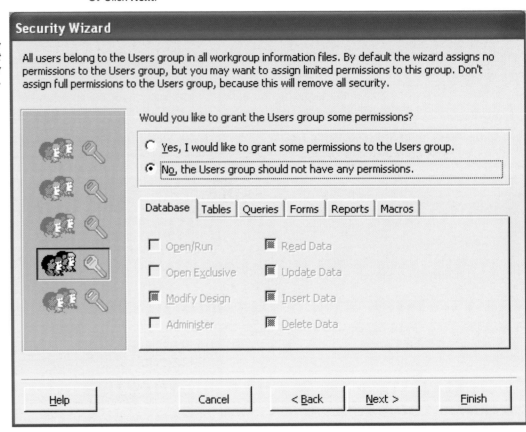

ADD, EDIT, AND REMOVE USERS

In the next Security Wizard dialog box, shown in Figure 9-6, you can get specific about which users to add to the workgroup. You can also delete a user from the workgroup and edit a user's password or PID.

Figure 9-6: The Security Wizard allows you to add users to and delete users from the workgroup.

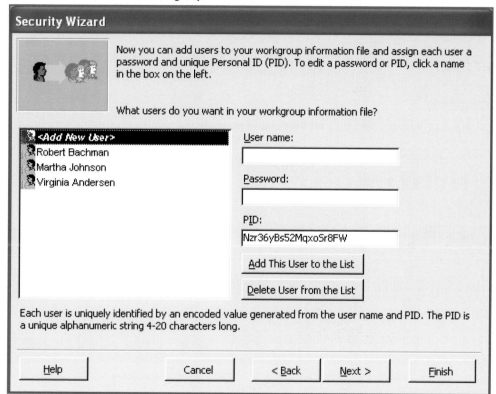

To add a new user:

1. Click **Add New User** in the left pane.

2. Type a name in the User Name text box.

3. Type a password in the Password text box.

4. The user's PID is automatically entered, but you can change it if you want to.

5. Click **Add This User To The List**.

6. Repeat Steps 1 through 5 to add other users to the workgroup.

To remove a user from the workgroup, select the name and click **Delete User From The List**. To edit user information, select the name and change the password or PID. Click **Next** when finished with the users in the workgroup.

ASSIGN USERS TO GROUPS

The final major step in defining user-level security is to assign each user to one of the groups that you have selected. You have two ways to carry this out in the next Security Wizard dialog box, as shown in Figure 9-7. You may start with a user and add the user to groups, or start with a group and assign users to it.

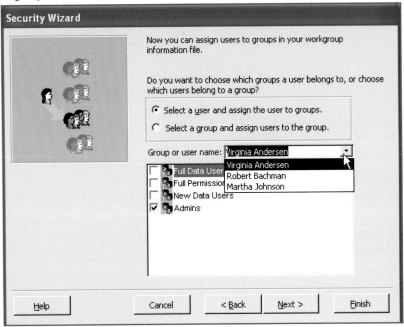

Figure 9-7: You can assign users to groups or groups to users.

1. In the next dialog box, click **Select A User And Assign The User To Groups**. The user names you added to the workgroup appear in the Group Or User Name drop-down list. The group names you included appear in the pane below the list.

2. Click the **Group Or User Name down arrow** and select a user name from the list.

3. In the lower pane, select each group name that you want the user to be a member of.

4. Repeat Steps 2 and 3 to assign other users to groups. Then click **Next**.

5. In the final Security Wizard dialog box, enter a name and path for the unsecured backup database, and click **Finish**.

SAVE OR PRINT THE SECURITY REPORT

It is extremely important to document and save all the security provisions you have set. When the Security Wizard is finished, a security report is displayed in Print Preview as shown in Figure 9-8. You will need all this information if you need to rebuild the WIF.

You have three ways to save the document:

- Click **Print** on the Print Preview toolbar to print a hardcopy of the report. Store the printout in a safe place.

- Choose **Tools | Office Links | Publish With Microsoft Office Word** to save it as a Word document. Print the document or store the file in a safe place.

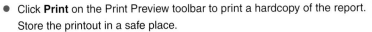

- Choose **File | Export** to open the Export Report *Reportname* As dialog box. In the Save As Type drop-down box, choose **Snapshot Format (*.snp)**, and type a name for the file in the File Name box. Click **Export**.

NOTE

You can assign a user to more than one group. The user then has all the permissions associated with all the groups she belongs to.

NOTE

When you assign users to groups in the Security Wizard, if you choose **Select A Group And Assign Users To The Group**, you select the group name in the **Group Or User Name** drop-down list and select the user names from the list below it.

9

QUICKSTEPS

KEEPING DATA SAFE

PREVENT USER ACCESS TO DATA IN A FORM

If you don't want the user to be able to get to a text box control in a form by pressing TAB:

1. Open the form in Design view.

2. Double-click the text box control you want to protect.

3. In the property sheet, click the **Other** tab.

4. Select the **Tab Stop** property, and choose **No** from the drop-down list. Then save the form design.

The user will still be able to click in the control and edit the contents.

Vertical	No
Auto Tab	No
Tab Stop	Yes
Tab Index	Yes
Shortcut Menu Bar	No

LIMIT TO VALUES IN A LOOKUP FIELD

A lookup field can appear in a form as a combo box or as a list box from which the user chooses a value. She may also enter a value not already on the list. If you don't want other values in the field:

1. Open the table in Design view.

2. Select the lookup field in the upper pane.

3. Click the **Lookup** tab in the lower pane, and change the Limit To List property to **Yes**.

General	Lookup		
Display Control	Combo Box		
Row Source Type	Value List		
Row Source	"Horses";"Dogs";"Cats";"Mice";"Turtles";"Goats"		
Bound Column	1		
Column Count	1		
Column Heads	No	Accept text only if it matches one of the listed
Column Widths	1"	choices?
List Rows	8	
List Width	1"	
Limit To List	Yes	
	No	

4. Save the table design.

Continued...

Figure 9-8: All the security provisions are documented in the security report.

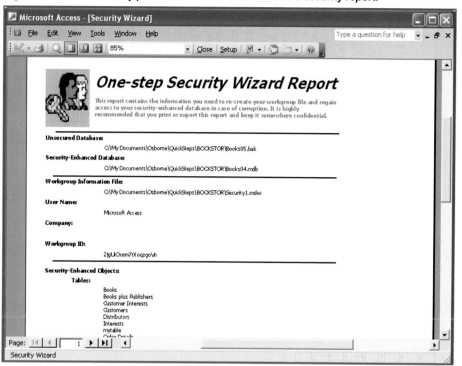

Apply Global Database Protection to a Database

Access offers several less comprehensive methods of securing a database and its objects. For example, you can require a password to open the database, and you can hide specific objects from user view. In addition, there are methods to create backup copies of the database and to improve performance by optimizing disk space usage.

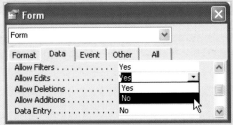
Use a Database Password

A database password only protects a database from being opened by someone who doesn't know the password. Anyone who knows the password can open the database. Once the database is open, the user can do anything with it.

ASSIGN A PASSWORD

You must have exclusive use of the database to assign a password.

To add a password, make sure all users have closed the database, then:

1. Click **File | Open**. In the Open dialog box, select the database, click the **Open down arrow**, and choose **Open Exclusive**.

2. Click **Tools | Security | Set Database Password**.

3. Type the password in the Password text box.

4. Repeat the password in the Verify text box, and then click **OK**. (If the entries don't match, Access will ask you to reenter the password in the Verify box. Do so, and click **OK**.)

The next time you try to open the database, you will be asked for the password.

Some basic guidelines for creating a password include:

- Create a password that combines uppercase and lowercase letters with numbers and symbols. This builds a "strong" password. For example, "67TrCg!89sdJ" is a strong password, while "MyFavoriteCat" is not.

- Never use a word that appears in the dictionary.
- Do not use the special characters that have a special meaning in Access: " \ [ ] : | < > + = ; , . ? *.

REMOVE A PASSWORD

To remove the requirement for a password:

1. Open the database in **Exclusive** mode.
2. Choose **Tools | Security | Unset Database Password**.
3. Enter the password and click **OK**.

ENCODE/DECODE A DATABASE

An *encoded* database is compacted and unreadable by any word processor or other utility program. You still have access to an encoded database and can work with it as usual. When you decode an encoded database, it returns to its original form.

The database must be closed before you can encode it. You must be the owner of the Workgroup Information File and be able to open it in Exclusive mode. In addition, your disk must have enough free space for both the original database and the encoded copy.

To encode a database:

1. In the empty Database window, click **Tools | Security | Encode/Decode Database**.
2. Select the database in the Encode/Decode Database dialog box, as shown in Figure 9-9, and click **OK**.
3. In the Encode Database As dialog box, specify the location where you want to save the encoded database, and click **Save**.

To decode the encoded database, repeat steps 1 and 2 above, and then specify the name and location in the Decode Database As dialog box. Click **OK**.

9

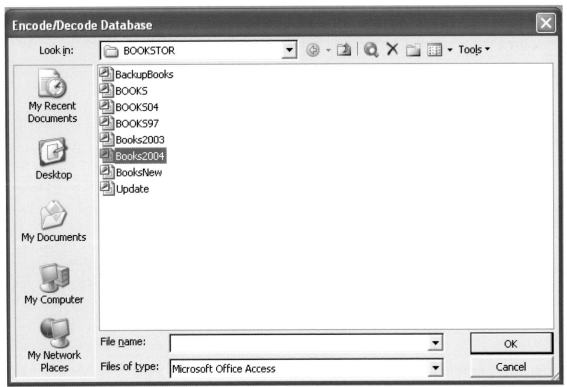

Figure 9-9: You can encode a database to make it unreadable by programs other than Access.

Remove Database Objects from View

Hiding database objects does not really tighten security; it just keeps certain objects from appearing in the Database window.

HIDE DATABASE OBJECTS

To hide an object:

1. Select the object in the Database window, and click **Properties** on the Database toolbar.

2. Check **Hidden** at the bottom of the General tab in the Properties dialog box, as shown in Figure 9-10.

3. Click **OK**.

> **NOTE**
>
> You can save the encoded version with the same name as the original, but you will be asked to confirm this. If the encode process fails, the original database is not deleted.

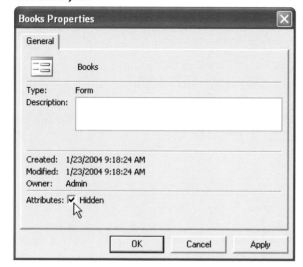

VIEW HIDDEN DATABASE OBJECTS

Normally, the hidden object is no longer listed in the Database window; however, you can choose to see the names of the hidden objects.

1. Choose **Tools | Options** and click the **View** tab.

2. In the Show area, select **Hidden Objects**.

3. Click **OK**.

Although the hidden objects appear dimmed in the Database window, they can still be opened. To remove the Hidden property, open the **Properties** dialog box (see the previous section, "Hide Database Objects") and deselect the **Hidden** option.

Back Up and Restore a Database

When working with an important database, it is a good idea to have a backup copy on hand. Creating a backup database on a regular basis can help reduce the risk of losing important data.

Before making a backup copy, make sure all users have closed their databases so all changes in the data have been saved.

You can make a backup copy from either outside or inside of Access. To backup without using Access, do one of the following:

- Right-click the file name in the Windows Explorer window, and point to **Send To** in the context menu, as shown in Figure 9-11. Click the drive where you want to save the copy.

- After locating the file name in the Windows Explorer window, drag it to another disk in the Folders pane.

- Use Microsoft Windows Backup and Recovery tools. For example, in Windows XP you can use the Automated System Recovery (ASR) tool (Click **Start | All Programs | Accessories | System Tools | Backup | Advanced Mode**). You can also use the MS-DOS Copy command or a third-party backup utility. (You may also be able to compress the file at the same time.)

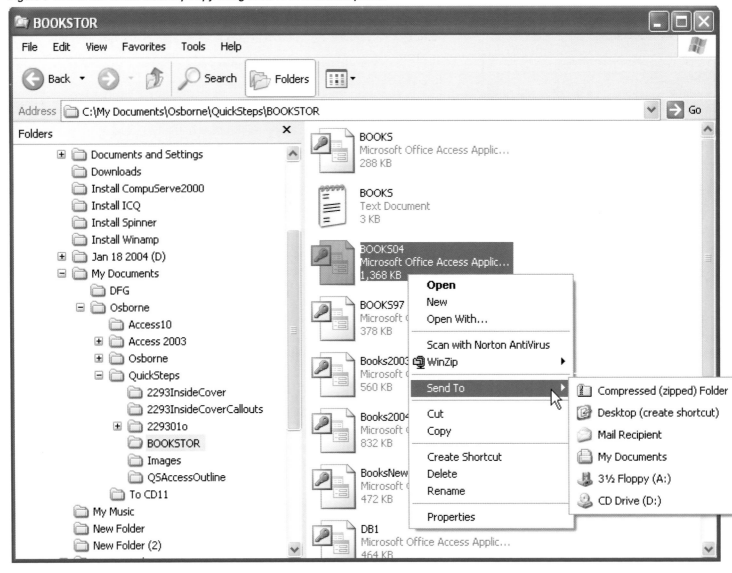

TIP

By default, the backup file keeps the same name with the current date added to it.

TIP

If yours is a multi-user environment, be sure to backup the Workgroup Information File, too.

BACK UP A DATABASE FROM ACCESS

You can use Access to create a regular copy to keep as a backup copy. No compression or other reformatting takes place—you just create a regular database file.

1. Click **File | Backup Database**.

2. Choose the location for the copy, and type a name for it in the Save Backup As dialog box, as shown in Figure 9-12.

3. Click **Save**.

Figure 9-12: You can also create a backup copy with Access.

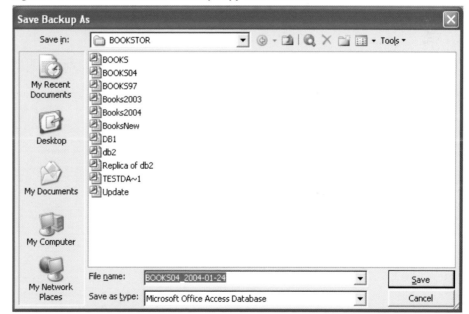

BACK UP INDIVIDUAL DATABASE OBJECTS

If you want to back up only a few objects instead of the whole database:

1. Create a new empty database.

2. Click **File | Get External Data | Import**.

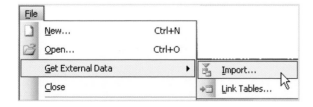

3. Locate and select the database in the Import dialog box. Click **Import**.

4. Click each tab in the Import Objects dialog box, as shown in Figure 9-13, and select the objects you want. See the section, "Import Data from Outside Sources," in Chapter 4 for more information about importing.

5. Click **OK** to import the objects.

6. Save the new database.

Figure 9-13: You can import objects into the backup database.

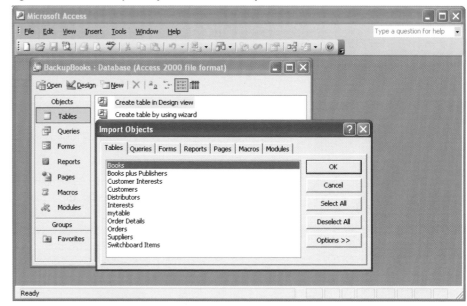

NOTE

By default, the new database assumes the Access 2000 format, unless you've changed the default settings. See Chapter 1 for more information about changing default settings.

TIP

Some definitions can cover many pages. Be sure to check how many before you start to print.

NOTE

You can save the Documenter's report as a Report Snapshot; an Excel worksheet; or in another format, such as HTML or RTF. (See Chapter 7 for information on creating a Report Snapshot.)

RESTORE A DATABASE

When you need to restore the database from the backup copy, use the recovery tool for the method you used to create the backup. For example, in Windows Explorer you may simply drag the file name back to the original folder on the hard drive.

Database Administration

Access provides tools to assist you in managing the size of your database, as well as to repair a database that may have become corrupted. You can also create a printout of your database relationships, database properties, and definitions of your database objects.

Figure 9-14: You can select just those objects you want documented.

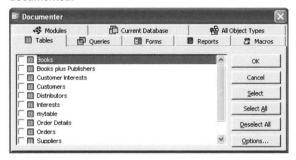

Document a Database

If you are working alone on your own database, you probably don't need extensive documentation of the database objects. In a corporation where there is a large information management team, documentation is extremely important. With up-to-date object definitions, errors can be quickly isolated and fixed.

The documentation can include all or a select group of objects in the database.

1. Choose **Tools | Analyze | Documenter**, as shown in Figure 9-14.

2. Either:

   - Select each object tab and select the objects you want documented, or click **Select All**.

   –Or–

   - Select the **All Objects Types** tab, and click **Select All**. This includes relationships and the database properties as well as the definitions of all the database objects.

3. If you don't need all the information about an object, you can click **Options** and choose how much you want to see. Figure 9-15 shows the choices you have with table documentation.

4. Click **OK** twice when you have finished making your selections.

5. When the Documenter is finished, the results appear in Print Preview.

6. Click **Print** to print the entire document, or press **CTRL+P** and use the Print dialog box to print selected pages. See Chapter 8 for more information on printing database objects.

Figure 9-15: Choose the table definition items to include in the documentation.

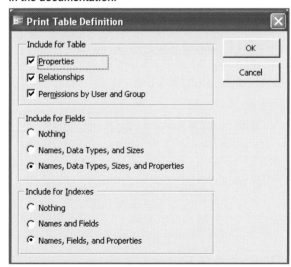

Compact and Repair a Database

Figure 9-16: Documenter shows you the documentation report before you print.

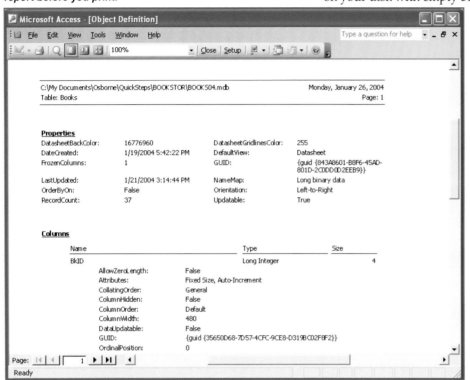

As you improve and modify your database, the file can become scattered about on your disk with empty blocks of space between. The *Compact and Repair Database* utility removes the empty spaces and rearranges the file more efficiently to improve performance. If there has been some damage, this utility can find the problems and offer to repair them at once.

You can start the compact and repair process with the database open or closed. With the database open, simply click **Tools | Database Utilities | Compact And Repair Database**.

If the database is closed, you can compact and repair it to the same file or with a different name in another location.

If the compact and repair utility doesn't work, one of the following problems may exist:

- The database may be open by another user. Wait for the other user to close the database and try again.

- There is not enough free space for both the original and the repaired database on the disk. Go back and delete unnecessary files, and try again.

- You may not have the required Open/Run and Open Exclusive permissions.

- The name of the database from an earlier version of Access may include a character that is no longer permitted, such as the grave accent (`). Return to the earlier version of Access, change the name, and then try again.

- The database file may be set to Read Only.

TIP

One of the options on the General tab of the Tools | Options dialog allows you to automatically compact a database when you close it if the reduction in size would be greater than 256K. To do this, select the **Compact On Close** option.

How to...

Chapter 10

Extending Access

The final chapter of this book will take you one step deeper into the advanced features of Access. You will analyze data by using a Crosstab query and PivotTables, link and export files, work with static and dynamic web pages, and create your own dialog box.

Use Advanced Data Analysis Tools

Access provides both basic and advanced tools to be used when analyzing and presenting data. This chapter will take you through a few of the advanced features, from using a Crosstab query to creating a Data Access Page.

Create a Crosstab Query with a Wizard

A Crosstab query presents information in a slightly different way than do the other queries. (See Chapter 5 for more information on Select and Action queries.) Rather than displaying the information in a standard datasheet format, the Crosstab query looks more like a spreadsheet, as shown in Figure 10-1. Calculated data and the values that make up that calculation reside in the body. The two descriptors for the values are displayed—one vertically in the column headings, the other horizontally in the row headings.

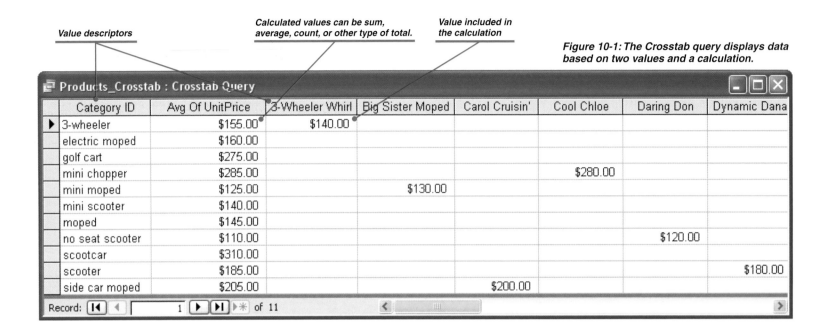

Value descriptors

Calculated values can be sum, average, count, or other type of total.

Value included in the calculation

Figure 10-1: The Crosstab query displays data based on two values and a calculation.

Category ID	Avg Of UnitPrice	3-Wheeler Whirl	Big Sister Moped	Carol Cruisin'	Cool Chloe	Daring Don	Dynamic Dana
3-wheeler	$155.00	$140.00					
electric moped	$160.00						
golf cart	$275.00						
mini chopper	$285.00				$280.00		
mini moped	$125.00		$130.00				
mini scooter	$140.00						
moped	$145.00						
no seat scooter	$110.00					$120.00	
scootcar	$310.00						
scooter	$185.00						$180.00
side car moped	$205.00			$200.00			

Record: ◀◀ ◀ 1 ▶ ▶▶ ▶* of 11

1. Open the Database window in the database you want to create the query.

2. Click **Queries** and then click **New** on the Database window toolbar.

3. In the New Query dialog box, select **Crosstab Query Wizard**, and click **OK**.

4. In the first dialog box of the Crosstab Query Wizard, click **Tables**, **Queries**, or **Both** to display the tables and/or queries in the database. Click the table or query where you first want to select the fields that will appear in your query results, and click **Next**.

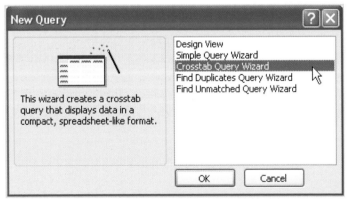

10

To include field names from more than one table in a Crosstab query, create a query combining all the field names you need and then use that query to create a Crosstab query.

5. In the next dialog box, as shown in Figure 10-2, choose the field(s) you want as row headings. Move the field(s) from the Available Fields to the Selected Fields list box. Double-click the fields you want, or use the select/remove buttons between the two list boxes to add or remove fields. Click **Next**.

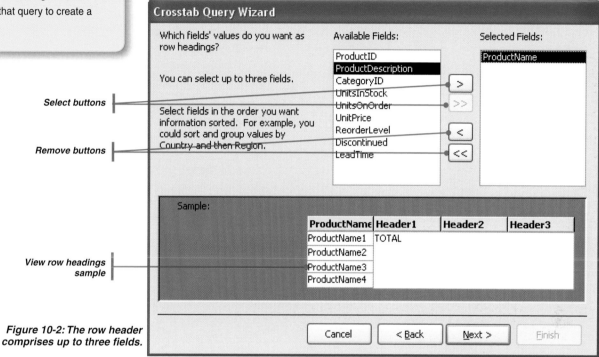

Select buttons

Remove buttons

View row headings sample

Figure 10-2: The row header comprises up to three fields.

6. The third step in the Crosstab Query Wizard is to select the field whose values you would like displayed as column headers. Click the field and click **Next**.

7. Click the field that you would like to make a calculated value. Click the function with which you would like to calculate the value. Select the **Yes, Include Row Sums** check box to display the row calculations. Click **Next**.

8. In the final dialog box, accept the default query name or type a title/name for the query.

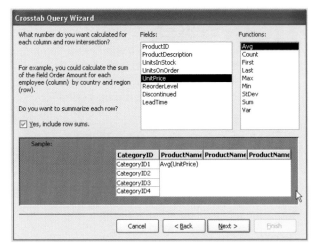

Choose whether to view (run) the query as is or to modify its design. If you need additional help, select the **Display Help On Working With The Crosstab Query** check box. Click **Finish** when done. Depending on your choice, the new Crosstab query will be displayed as a datasheet with fields you selected earlier in the wizard, shown in Figure 10-1, or it will open in Design view, ready for adding criteria and other changes. In either case, the new query will be listed under Queries in the Database window.

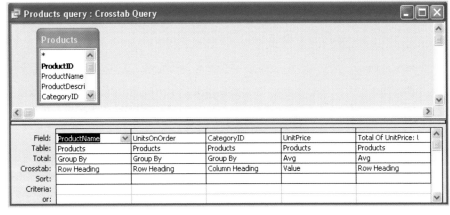

Create a PivotTable in Forms

PivotTables allow you to present your data in an easily understood format. You can dynamically change the layout of a PivotTable to analyze data in different ways. You can move row headings, column headings, and page fields until you achieve the desired layout. Each time you change the layout, the PivotTable immediately recalculates the data based on the new design. A wizard helps you create the initial PivotTable form and lets you quickly make changes that pivot the table.

TIP

To quickly create a PivotTable based on one table or query, use Autoform:PivotTable. Click **New** on the Database toolbar and select **Autoform:PivotTable**. Select a table by clicking the **down arrow** at the bottom right side of the dialog box. A PivotTable will be created, awaiting your layout input.

NOTE

Fields from multiple tables must come from related tables (see "Relate Tables," in Chapter 2). If the tables have no relationship, an alert message will appear.

1. Open the Database window in the database for which you want to create the PivotTable.

2. Click **Forms** and then click **New** on the Database window toolbar.

3. In the New Form dialog box, select **PivotTable Wizard**. Select the table or query you want as the basis for your PivotTable, and click **OK**.

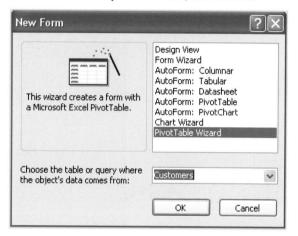

4. The first dialog box displays a message defining the PivotTable object. Click **Next**.

5. In the last dialog box of the PivotTable Wizard, shown in Figure 10-3, click the **Table/Queries down arrow** and choose a table or query where you first want to select the fields that will appear in your PivotTable. Move the fields you want from the Available Fields to the Fields Chosen For Pivoting list box. Double-click the fields you want, or use the select/remove buttons between the two list boxes to add or remove the fields.

Figure 10-3: Choose fields from your data source that you will "pivot" to produce new analysis opportunities.

Select one or all fields.

Remove one or all fields.

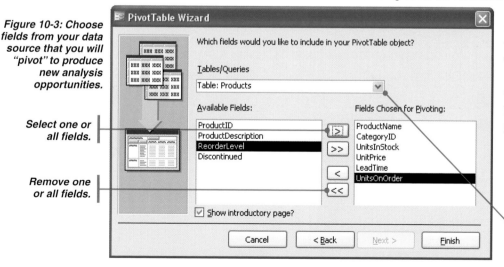

Click the drop down arrow to choose other Tables/Queries.

NOTE

If the table or query you choose to base your PivotTable on doesn't have all the fields you need, don't worry. The second dialog box will present the opportunity to select fields from any table or query within your database.

TIP

Liberally select your fields for the PivotTable. This allows you to choose from many fields to display in the PivotTable during data analysis.

TIP

To move fields to the PivotTable from the PivotTable list box, you can either drag the field from the field list to the PivotTable area, or select the field within the PivotTable list box and click the **down arrow** to select the field location from within the PivotTable List box. Click **Add to**, and your selected field will appear in your chosen location.

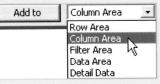

6. Repeat Steps 4 and 5 if you want to include fields from other tables or queries. Click **Finish** when finished adding fields. A blank layout area and field name list box is now displayed, as shown in Figure 10-4.

Figure 10-4: Data within the PivotTable can be pivoted to provide new analysis opportunities.

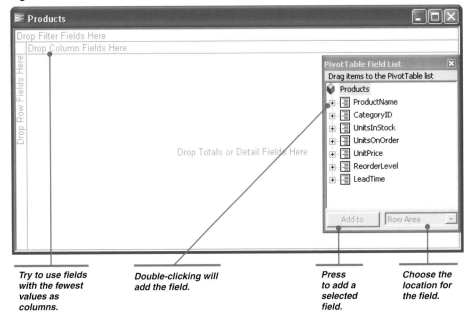

Try to use fields with the fewest values as columns.

Double-clicking will add the field.

Press to add a selected field.

Choose the location for the field.

Create the PivotTable Layout

1. Use the PivotTable Wizard to create a blank layout area, similar to Figure 10-4.

2. Drag an item from the PivotTable Field list to one of the boxes listed below, according to what you want to do.

- **Drop Row Fields Here** allows you to display each category of that item in its own row. Typically, these items are descriptive and identifying, not numerical—for example, Country, Salesperson, and Title.

- **Drop Column Fields Here** allows you to display each category of the item in its own column. Typically, these items are descriptive and identifying, not numerical—for example, Category or Product Name.

- **Drop Totals or Detail Fields Here** allows you to sum or otherwise perform calculations and display the results. Typically, these items are numerical and capable of being counted, summed, and calculated.

- **Drop Filter Fields Here** allows you to filter the view to a particular part of the data. For example, if your PivotTable displays information regarding your product line, you can place the field named Categories in the **Drop Filter Fields Here** area to display only the product line within selected categories.

3. Repeat Step 2 to create the layout that displays the information you want. You can drop more than one item in a box, and you can drag an item from a box to outside the layout area to remove it. See Figure 10-5 for an example of using multiple PivotTable Field list items in a row field arrangement.

Figure 10-5: Pivot the table by dragging fields to different PivotTable locations.

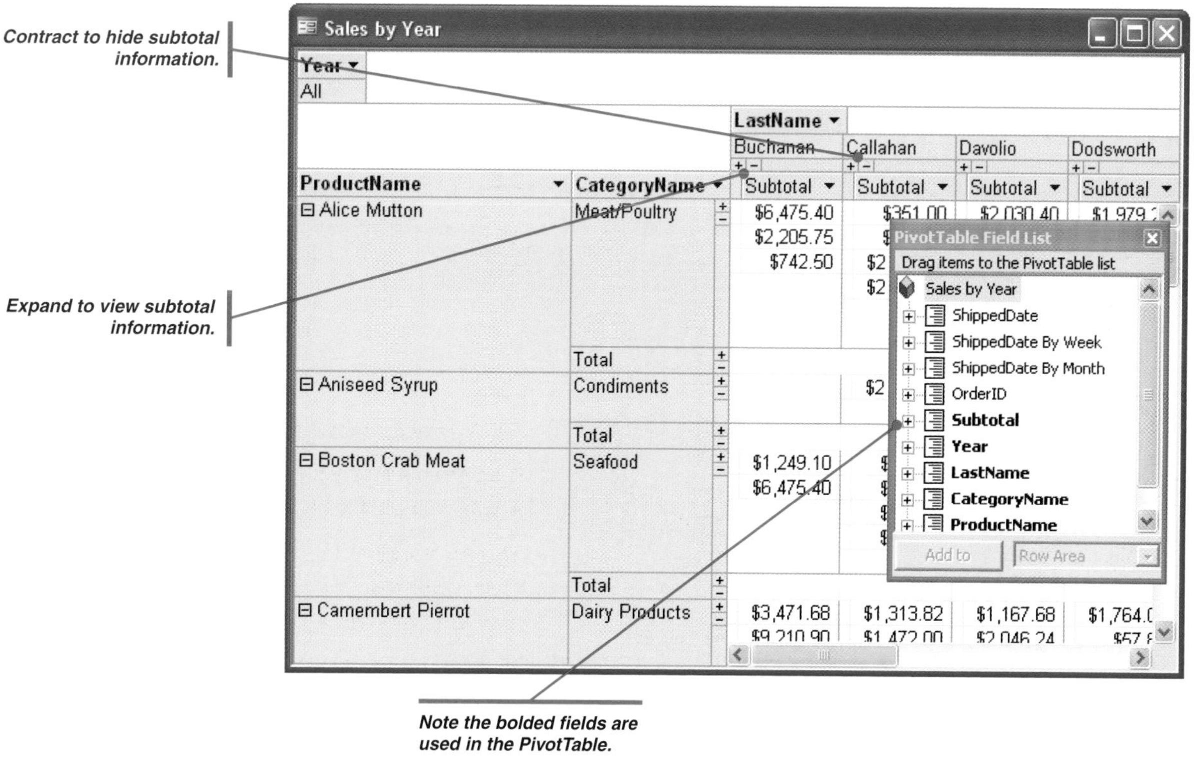

Contract to hide subtotal information.

Expand to view subtotal information.

Note the bolded fields are used in the PivotTable.

TIP

You can also switch any table, form, or query to PivotTable or PivotChart view by clicking the **View down arrow** and selecting the desired view.

NOTE

More information on PivotCharts and on charting in general is offered in *Microsoft Office Excel 2003 QuickSteps*, published by McGraw-Hill/Osborne.

Figure 10-6: PivotCharts utilize the same method of moving fields as do PivotTables.

Create a PivotChart

PivotCharts provide the same ability to dynamically change data as do PivotTables, but in a chart format. The creation method is just as simple as for PivotTables.

1. Open the Database window in the database for which you want to create the PivotChart.

2. Click **Forms** and then click **New** on the Database window toolbar.

3. In the New Forms dialog box, select **Autoform: PivotChart**. Select the table or query you want as the basis for your PivotChart, and click **OK**. The PivotChart blank layout area will be displayed, as shown in Figure 10-6, with a field list containing all the fields from the chosen table or query.

4. Drag items from the PivotChart Field list to the applicable chart areas on the PivotChart layout to build the chart, as shown in Figure 10-7. Pivot the different values to analyze your data from a visual standpoint.

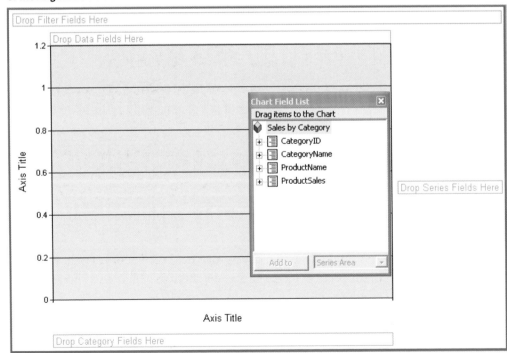

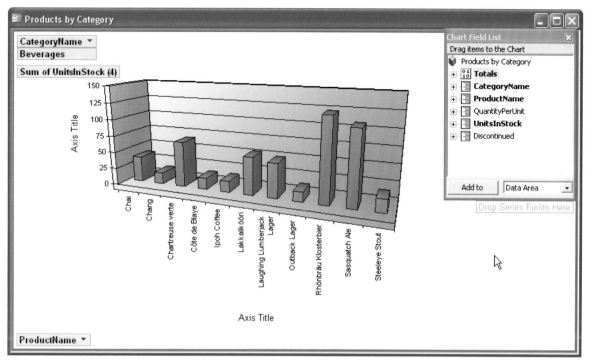

Figure 10-7: Manipulate the values in the PivotChart to highlight different values.

Share Data

Sharing data is an essential element of any workplace environment. This section will take you through exporting and linking Access data to a variety of applications.

Export Access Data

Just as you can import data from other programs (see "Import Data From Outside Sources," in Chapter 4), you can export Access objects to a variety of other data formats.

1. Open the Database window in the database whose objects you would like to export.

2. Click the table, query, form, report, or page you would like to export.

TABLE 10-1: OBJECT EXPORT FORMATS

OBJECT	EXPORT FORMAT
Table	Access, dBASE, Excel, HTML, Lotus 1-2-3, Paradox, Text, SharePoint Team Services, Active Server Pages, Microsoft Internet Information Server, Rich Text Format, Word Merge, XML, Open Database Connectivity
Query	Access, dBASE, Excel, HTML, Lotus 1-2-3, Paradox, Text, SharePoint Team Services, Active Server Pages, Microsoft Internet Information Server, Rich Text Format, Word Merge, XML, Open Database Connectivity
Form	Access, Excel, HTML, Text, Active Server Pages, Microsoft Internet Information Server, Rich Text Format, XML
Report	Access, Excel, HTML, Text, Rich Text Format, Snapshot, XML
Page	Access, Data Access Page

3. Select **File | Export** to open the Export To dialog box. Table 10-1 provides a view of the export formats available to each object.

4. Click the **Save In down arrow** to choose a location to in which save the exported file.

5. Click the **Save As Type down arrow** and select the file format in which you want to export your data.

6. Type a file name in the text box, and click **Export**. To view the exported file, go to the location where you saved the file and open it in the format's corresponding application, as shown in Figure 10-8.

Link Files

Access can *link*, or connect, data in multiple Access databases as well as between Access databases and other applications. It doesn't matter whether that data resides on your machine or on a network.

Figure 10-8: Tables and spreadsheets, though similar in appearance, differ in functionality.

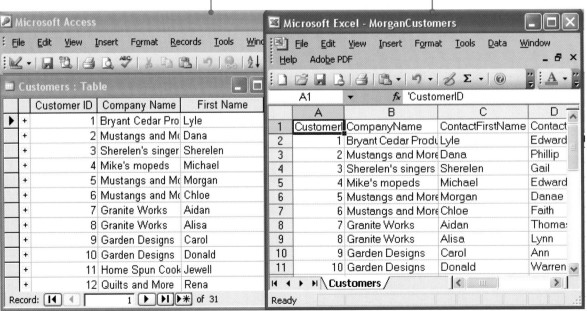

Access table from which exported Excel file was created

Exported Excel file

WORKING WITH OFFICELINKS

When your knowledge base lies in a Microsoft Office application other than Access, it is sometimes faster and easier to take the data from an Access object and work with it using your familiar tools. Access provides a great means of doing just this by using OfficeLinks with your tables and queries.

MERGE WITH MICROSOFT WORD

Use the OfficeLinks feature if, for example, you have a customer address table within Access and would like to merge it with a Word document.

1. Open the Database window in the database whose table or query you would like to use.

2. Click a table or query (for example, a customer address table), and click the **OfficeLinks down arrow** on the Database toolbar. A menu of three possible commands is displayed.

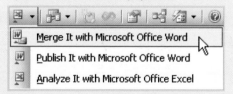

3. Click **Merge It With Microsoft Office Word**. This will launch Microsoft Word and start the Mail Merge Wizard.

4. Follow the wizard to create your merged document using Access data.

PUBLISH WITH MICROSOFT WORD

To take the contents of a table or query and work with it as you would a standard Word document:

1. Open the Database window in the database whose table or query you would like to use.

2. Click on the database object you would like to use in Word, and click the **OfficeLinks down arrow** on the toolbar.

Continued...

You can link data formatted as a table, text, or spreadsheet and process it with queries, forms, and reports in your database. The downside to using links primarily revolves around speed: you will probably notice the database is a bit slower than if all the data were to reside within your database. The advantages, however, lie in your ability to link data that is shared between many users or stored on a host computer.

LINK TABLES

You can link to tables in Access files or those from several other database programs.

1. Open the Database window of the database to which you would like to link table(s). Click **File | Get External Data | Link Tables**. The Link dialog box will be displayed.

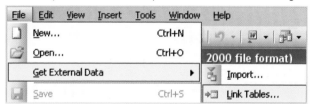

2. In the Look In box, browse to find the database you would like to link to your current database. Select that database and click **Link** to display the list of tables in the database.

3. Select one or more tables, and click **OK** to link the tables to your current database. Access marks the icon for linked tables in the Database window with an arrow.

WORKING WITH OFFICELINKS

(Continued)

3. Click **Publish It With Microsoft Office Word**. The selected object will automatically be displayed as a Word document.

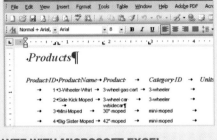

ANALYZE WITH MICROSOFT EXCEL

If Excel is your primary tool of choice, quickly send a table or query to Excel using the OfficeLinks button.

Open the database as described above in the first QuickSteps.

1. Open the Database window in the database whose table or query you would like to use.

2. Click the database object you would like to use in Excel, and click the **OfficeLinks down arrow** on the toolbar.

3. Click **Analyze It With Microsoft Office Excel**. The selected object will automatically be displayed within an Excel worksheet.

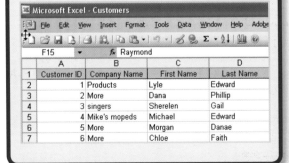

LINK TEXT AND SPREADSHEET FILES

1. Open the Database window of the database to be linked. Click **File | Get External Data | Link Tables**. The Link dialog box will be displayed.

2. Select the type of file you would like to link to from the File Of Type drop-down list.

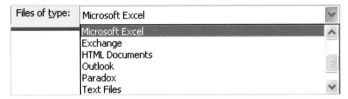

3. In the Look In box, browse to find the spreadsheet or text file you would like to link to. Select that file and click **Link** to launch the Link Spreadsheet Wizard, as shown in Figure 10-9, or the Link Text Wizard. Follow the steps in the wizard, which are the same as when importing a spreadsheet or text file. See "Import Data From Outside Sources" in Chapter 4, for information on importing spreadsheets and text files.

Figure 10-9: Use the Link Spreadsheet or Link Text Wizard when linking non-database data.

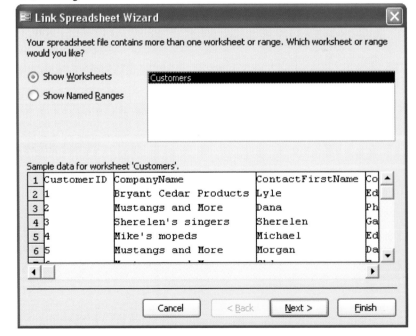

Integrate Web technology

The Internet has done a great job of connecting people and information. Access taps into Web technology in a variety of ways.

You can create a *hyperlink*, a direct link providing direct access from one object to another, within an Access table to connect users to information in the World Wide Web or elsewhere. Existing database objects can be saved as static web pages that provide access to data from a variety of locations and using different tools. Data access pages (or *pages*) are created within Access and allow Internet and intranet users to view and work with data that is stored in an Access database.

Add a Hyperlink Field to an Existing Table

To create a hyperlink within a table, you need to establish the field data type as a hyperlink. Hyperlink data type lets you store simple or complex links to files or documents outside your database. The "pointer" can contain a Uniform Resource Locator (URL) that points to a location on the World Wide Web or to a place on a local intranet. It can also use a file address to provide access to a file on your computer or in a server on your network.

1. In the database that will hold your newly created hyperlink(s), open the table in Design view.

2. Click in the first available field at the bottom of the Field Names column. Type a name for your new hyperlink field name.

3. Click the **Data Type down arrow** and select **Hyperlink**. Type a description for your new field in the description box and click **Save** on the Database toolbar. Data typed into the new field will be underlined and ready to search for the hyperlinked location.

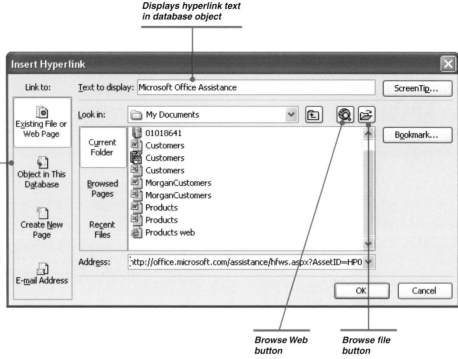

Displays hyperlink text
in database object

Figure 10-10: The hyperlink dialog box
provides a means to link data residing
at various locations.

Dialog box options will
change based on the
"Link To" selection.

Browse Web
button

Browse file
button

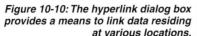**QUICKSTEPS**

CREATING A HYPERLINK TO A FILE OR WEB PAGE

Placing a hyperlink in a form or report is a great way to connect data from files or the Internet to the information displayed in your form or report.

1. Open your form or report in Design view, and select the **Insert Hyperlink** button. The Insert Hyperlink dialog box will be displayed, as shown in Figure 10-10.

2. In the Link To column, click **Existing File** or **Web Page**. Click either the **Browse Web** or the **Browse File** button to find the file or web page to which you would like to link.

3. Type the text you would like displayed to represent the hyperlink in the Text To Display text box. Click **OK**. You will return to Design view. Drag your new hyperlink control to the appropriate location within the form or report.

Save Database Objects as Static Web Pages

The quickest way to publish some or all of your database objects to a web page is to export your data as an *HTML* (Hypertext Markup Language) file. While this type of file presents a static view of your data, it can be easily posted to a web site.

1. Open your database to the Database window and select the object you would like to make a static web page.

2. Click **File | Export**. The Export Dialog box is displayed.

Save as type:	HTML Documents
	Microsoft Excel 5-7
	Microsoft Excel 97-2003
	HTML Documents
	Lotus 1-2-3 WJ2
	Lotus 1-2-3 WK1
	Lotus 1-2-3 WK3

TIP

If you select the **Autostart** check box within the File Export Dialog box, your static web page will display automatically after clicking **Export**.

3. Click the **Save As Type down arrow**, and select **HTML Documents**. Browse to the location where you would like to save this page, and type a file name in the File Name text box. If you are exporting a table or query, you can click the **Save Formatted** check box, which will allow you to use an existing HTML template to establish formats.

4. Click **Export**. If the **Save Formatted** check box is selected, the HTML Output Options dialog box will appear after clicking Export. Browse to find the HTML template holding the display options and click **OK**.

5. Go to the location where you saved the HTML document and open it to see the result, as shown in Figure 10-11.

Figure 10-11: The static web page provides detail without much design.

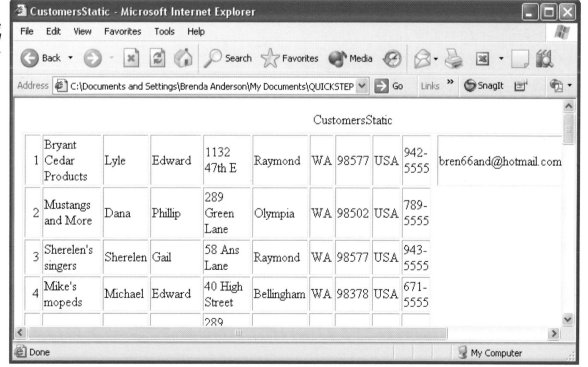

CustomersStatic

1	Bryant Cedar Products	Lyle	Edward	1132 47th E	Raymond	WA	98577	USA	942-5555	bren66and@hotmail.com
2	Mustangs and More	Dana	Phillip	289 Green Lane	Olympia	WA	98502	USA	789-5555	
3	Sherelen's singers	Sherelen	Gail	58 Ans Lane	Raymond	WA	98577	USA	943-5555	
4	Mike's mopeds	Michael	Edward	40 High Street	Bellingham	WA	98378	USA	671-5555	

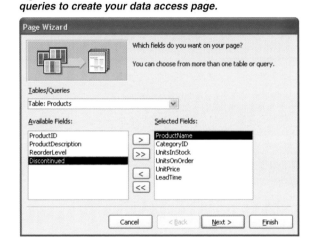

Figure 10-12: Choose fields from multiple tables and queries to create your data access page.

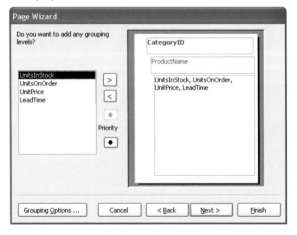

Figure 10-13: Establish grouping levels that will be used to display data order.

Create a Data Access Page with a Wizard

Data access pages are a special type of HTML form page that can navigate, filter, and update data in your database.

1. Open a database and click the **Pages** object in the Database window. Double-click **Create Data Access Page By Using Wizard**. This will launch the Page Wizard.

2. In the first dialog box of the Page Wizard, shown in Figure 10-12, click the **Tables/ Queries down arrow**, and then choose the table or query where you first want to select the fields that will appear on your page.

3. Move the fields you want from the Available Fields to the Selected Fields list box. Double-click the fields you want, or use the select/remove buttons between the two list boxes to add or remove fields.

4. Repeat Steps 2 and 3 if you want to include fields from other tables or queries. Click **Next** when finished adding fields.

5. The second step of the wizard provides an opportunity to establish grouping levels. Double-click the fields you want to group under, as shown in Figure 10-13, or select the fields and click the **right arrow**. Click **Next** when grouping levels are selected.

6. In the wizard's next dialog box, specify any additional sort order for the detail fields. Click the **down arrow** in the first sort order box and select any fields you wish to have in a sorted order. Continue this process through the sort order boxes until you have met your criteria. Click **Next**.

7. In the final dialog box, type a title/name for the page and choose whether to open the page as is or modify its design. If you would like to apply a theme to your page, choose the modify option and select the **Do You Want To Apply A Theme To Your Page?** check box. Click **Finish**. If the check box is selected, the Theme dialog box will be displayed, as shown in Figure 10-14; if not, the chosen view will be displayed. Click through the sample themes on the left side of the dialog box to choose one that fits your situation. Select a style and click **OK** to return to your data access page in Design view. Click **View | Web Page Preview** to view your Page as it would appear on the Internet, as shown in Figure 10-15

Figure 10-14: Apply a theme to jazz up your page.

Figure 10-15: The data access page, including an optional theme, can be edited in Design view.

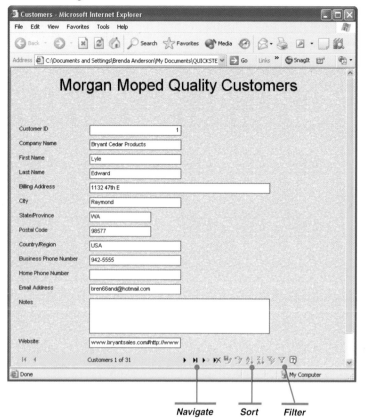

Navigate   Sort   Filter

NOTE

Users need to have Microsoft Internet Explorer 5.0 or later to view data access pages.

TIP

You can navigate through, sort, filter and perform other actions on data access pages using the tools at the bottom of the page.

Create a User Interface

When you create a database intended to be used by less experienced Access users, you can create interfaces that clearly offer a choice of activities. You can make your own custom dialog boxes, in which the user can click a button to open a form, preview a report, or perform nearly any other action.

Create a Custom Dialog Box

A dialog box is a special type of window that stays on the screen until you respond, even if only to close the window. The New Form dialog box is a good example of a built-in dialog box: you select a method of creating the form, and click **OK** or click **Cancel**. Figure 10-16 shows a custom dialog box made for a Books database.

To build your own dialog box, open a new form and add command buttons with the help of the Command Button Wizard. After adding the controls, you can change some of the form properties so it behaves like a popup dialog box.

Figure 10-16: A custom dialog box offers a set of actions to pursue.

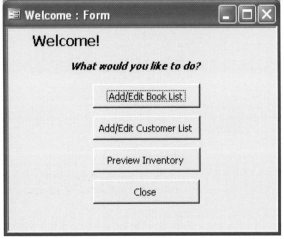

Add Command Button Controls to a Dialog Box

1. Click **Forms** and select **New** on the database toolbar. Click **Design view** to open a blank form.
2. Click the **Toolbox** button to open it.
3. Make sure the Control Wizards button is selected, and click the **Command Button** tool.
4. Click in the form design to place your command button.
5. Use the Command Button Wizard to choose the desired response to the button click. See "Add A Command Button" in Chapter 6 for details.
6. Enter a text label for the button.
7. Repeat Steps 3 through 6 to add the rest of the buttons.

Set Dialog Box Properties

In order for the form to behave as a pop-up form, you need to set the properties.

1. Click **Properties** on the forms toolbar to open the Properties dialog box.
2. If you want the title bar to show other than the form name, type the title as the Caption.
3. Set Default View to **Single Form**.
4. Set Allow Form View to **Yes**, but set the other three Allow properties to **No**.
5. Set Scroll Bars to **Neither**.
6. Set Record Selectors, Navigation Buttons, and Dividing Lines to **No**.
7. Set AutoResize and AutoCenter to **Yes**.

CAUTION

Be sure to either include an option that closes the pop-up form or keep the Control Box property set to **Yes**. If you don't, you won't be able to close the form!

adjust column width, 96-97
adjust row height, 99
create shortcuts, 9
image sizing, 169
move a column, 98
resize object windows, 15
select records, fields and columns, 80-81

N

Northwind Sample Database, 9

O

objects
  bound/unbound, 168
  database, saving as static Web pages,
    218-219
  defined, 3-5
  existing, inserting, 170, 171
  export formats, 214
  individual, securing, 189, 201
  rearrange, 15
  OfficeLinks, 215-216
opening
  databases, 5-9
  Help, 18
  recently used databases, 7
  shortcuts, 9
  using Dialog box, 6
  using Windows Explorer, 7
option groups, 133, 136-137

P

page breaks, 159
page numbers, 159
page printing, 181, 184-185, 186
page setup, 176, 177, 178, 179, 180, 181, 182,
  184-185
Page Wizard, 220
passwords, 196-197
PDFs, 184, 185
personal IDs (PIDs), 188
personalizing
  Access, 12-17

toolbars, 14
pictures
  adding, 133, 134
  objects, bound/unbound, 168
  using Database Wizard, 26
  using Insert Object, 80
  See also images
PivotChart, 123, 212-213
PivotTable, 123, 209, 210
PivotTable Wizard, 209, 210-211
primary key
  assigning, 37, 44
  changing fields, 44
  creating, 40, 44
  establishing, 36
  inserting into "keyless" table, 44
  referential integrity, enforcing, 48
  relationships, 45-47
  tables, relating, 46-47
printer, choosing, 178, 184, 185
printing
  choosing, 178, 184-185
  columnar settings, changing, 179-180
  copies, multiple, 186
  documentation, 194-195, 202, 203-204
  Help topic, 18
  landscape, 177
  margins, adjusting, 177
  pages, choosing and setup, 176-186
  paper, change layout, size and source, 177
  portrait, 177
  preview, 180-183
  security reports, 194-195
  setting up, 176
  to a file, 184
print preview, 148, 149, 150, 194, 202
properties, 119; 120; 130, 144, 145, 168, 174,
  175, 178, 196, 198, 199, 203, 222

Q

queries
  crosstab, 205-208
  defined, 3, 113
  modifying, 115
  properties, setting, 119-120
  saving, 118
  Simple Query Wizard, 113-118
  stopping, 118

types, 5:13
viewing, 118
working in design view, 116
working in grid view, 117
Quick Launch, 2, 9

R

read-only, deselecting, 30, 50
Recently Used File List, changing, 8
records
  copy, 82
  defined, 3, 21, 22
  deleting, 83
  displaying, 107
  identifying, 37, 44
  moving, 78, 82
  relationships, 38, 44, 48
  saving, 60
  selecting, 80-81
  sorting, 102-103, 104
  See also filter
referential integrity, enforcing, 48
relationships, 45-47, 181, 183
reports
  AutoReport, 149-150
  common tasks, 159
  customizing, 25
  design, modifying, 174-176
  Design view, 154-156
  information, grouping and sorting, 152-153
  labels, 162-164
  layout/style, 154
  modifying, 157-159
  pictures, inserting, 26
  Report Wizard, 150-154
  sections, 155
  security, saving/printing, 194-195
  snapshot, 164-165, 202
  snapshot, distributing, 166
  subreports, 160-162
  titles, 26; 154
  tools, 156
  values, calculating, 158-159
  viewing, 27, 148-149
  See also Design view
  See also printing
restoring, 199-200, 202
row height, adjusting, 99

International Contact Information

AUSTRALIA
McGraw-Hill Book Company Australia Pty. Ltd.
TEL +61-2-9900-1800
FAX +61-2-9878-8881
http://www.mcgraw-hill.com.au
books-it_sydney@mcgraw-hill.com

CANADA
McGraw-Hill Ryerson Ltd.
TEL +905-430-5000
FAX +905-430-5020
http://www.mcgraw-hill.ca

GREECE, MIDDLE EAST, & AFRICA
(Excluding South Africa)
McGraw-Hill Hellas
TEL +30-210-6560-990
TEL +30-210-6560-993
TEL +30-210-6560-994
FAX +30-210-6545-525

MEXICO (Also serving Latin America)
McGraw-Hill Interamericana Editores S.A. de C.V.
TEL +525-1500-5108
FAX +525-117-1589
http://www.mcgraw-hill.com.mx
carlos_ruiz@mcgraw-hill.com

SINGAPORE (Serving Asia)
McGraw-Hill Book Company
TEL +65-6863-1580
FAX +65-6862-3354
http://www.mcgraw-hill.com.sg
mghasia@mcgraw-hill.com

SOUTH AFRICA
McGraw-Hill South Africa
TEL +27-11-622-7512
FAX +27-11-622-9045
robyn_swanepoel@mcgraw-hill.com

SPAIN
McGraw-Hill/Interamericana de España, S.A.U.
TEL +34-91-180-3000
FAX +34-91-372-8513
http://www.mcgraw-hill.es
professional@mcgraw-hill.es

**UNITED KINGDOM, NORTHERN,
EASTERN, & CENTRAL EUROPE**
McGraw-Hill Education Europe
TEL +44-1-628-502500
FAX +44-1-628-770224
http://www.mcgraw-hill.co.uk
emea_queries@mcgraw-hill.com

ALL OTHER INQUIRIES Contact:
McGraw-Hill/Osborne
TEL +1-510-420-7700
FAX +1-510-420-7703
http://www.osborne.com
omg_international@mcgraw-hill.com